LOST GREEN BAY

KRIS LEONHARDT

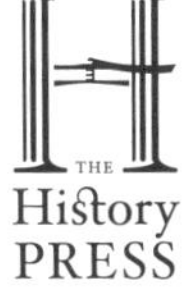

Published by The History Press
An imprint of Arcadia Publishing
Charleston, SC
www.historypress.com

First published 2026

Manufactured in the United States

ISBN 9781467158367

Library of Congress Control Number: 2025945977

Notice: The information in this book is true and complete to the best of our knowledge. It is offered without guarantee on the part of the author or The History Press. The author and The History Press disclaim all liability in connection with the use of this book.

CONTENTS

Chapter 1

THE RISE AND DECLINE OF THE ST. JOSEPH'S ORPHANAGE

The first orphanage in America was established in the 1700s to care for deserted children as the incoming Europeans and other immigrants faced conflict while trying to settle land already inhabited.

Orphanages grew in the early 1800s as charitable groups looked to care for children orphaned as a result of health epidemics, conflict, and struggling to make it in a new world. The financial struggles of the Depression era exacerbated the issue, setting it on a trajectory to reach an all-time high.

"In the 30 years following the end of World War II, both the number of orphanages in America and the number of children in them declined dramatically. Nationally, the number of children in institutional care fell from a high of approximately 144,000 in the mid-1930s to 95,000 in 1951 and 63,000 in 1970," Marshall B. Jones wrote in the "Crisis of the American Orphanage, 1931–40" for Pennsylvania State University.

The rise and fall of the country's orphanages is mirrored in the lifespan of Green Bay's St. Joseph's Orphan Asylum (later known as St. Joseph's Home). The Catholic facility was opened as an orphanage on June 29, 1877, under the direction of Bishop Joseph Melcher, Sister Melania, and Father Norbert Kersten at the corner of Webster Street and Crooks Street in Green Bay with six children and assistance from the Notre Dame Sisters of Milwaukee.

In a little over a year, the orphanage had thirty-four children residing there. A report to the State Board of Charities and Reforms for the year 1881 showed seventy-five children in the facility: twenty-seven taken in, twenty-four discharged, one death, and two runaways—all but two from northeastern Wisconsin. An 1887 report showed one hundred orphans and six boarders—fifty-eight boys and forty-eight girls—with fourteen in the nursery. In 1889, plans for a boys' home were announced.

An existing farm was later purchased on Riverside Drive just north of St. Joseph's Street, and a large historic Italianate residence was built in 1896. The large, imposing structure drew the attention of those passing by the facility.

"A new gate has been put up along the street car track at St. Joseph's Orphan Asylum. Over it is placed the words, 'St. Joseph's Orphan Asylum.' This is done so that strangers going to De Pere can tell what the institution is," an August 1900 *Green Bay Semi-Weekly Gazette* article stated.

And the orphan population was starting to outgrow its capacity. "The St. Joseph Orphan Asylum, it is expected will in the course of the next few days have 200 inmates," a March 10, 1900 *Green Bay Semi-Weekly Gazette* article read. "There are today 193 children in the institution, six having been received the last of this week or the first of next.

"Accommodations at the St. Joseph's Asylum are now being taxed to their utmost."

In 1902, a south wing was added, but the orphan population continued to grow, getting as high as three hundred, with a staff of fifty priests and nuns, before starting to decline.

A ROOF OVER THEIR HEADS

The 1909 White House Conference on the Care of Dependent Children initiated by President Theodore Roosevelt brought together social workers, educators, juvenile court judges, and other civic leaders in opposition to the institutionalization of neglected and orphaned children. The conference led to the creation of the Children's Bureau, the widows' pension movement, and the growth of adoption agencies.

Marian J. Morton wrote in "Surviving the Great Depression" for John Carroll University:

> *At the 1930 White House Conference on Child Health and Protection, Home Folks, a long-time critic of orphanages, reported that 220,000 needy children remained in "their own homes," thanks to state mother's pensions; these allowed women to care for their children at home rather*

> *than place them in orphanages. At long last, Folks hoped, professional social workers were able to implement the "fundamental principles of social work" articulated at the 1909 White House Conference on Dependent Children: most significantly, "home life is the highest and finest product of civilization....Except in unusual circumstances, the home should not be broken up for reasons of poverty." But the nation had already descended into the Great Depression, an "unusual circumstance" that devastated families and moved thousands of children into foster homes and orphanages.*

One of those children affected by "unusual circumstances" was June Muller, now ninety-one and living in the Green Bay area.

"I was about twelve years old when my sister and I were placed in the orphanage because my mother couldn't take care of us and nobody else in their family," recalled Muller, whose father had died young from cancer.

Muller and her sister, JoAnn, were born in Illinois, but after their dad's passing, their mother moved them to Wisconsin, where she hoped that the girls' grandmother could assist. "And she couldn't take care of us; so, she put us in the orphanage to have a place to keep us until she could find a job and an apartment," Muller added.

Muller and her sister were placed at the St. Joseph's Orphanage.

"We were away from our mother and we kept being told that my mother was coming to get us," Muller said.

"We had to put up with the rules and regulations; it was run by nuns and priests. There were a lot of other kids that were running away that had no place to go that were also placed in the orphanage. We all had chores to do, and we all had like serial numbers in our clothes so they knew who we were, and we all went to church every day.

"The orphanage wasn't the sweetest place to be, believe me. It was the place that took care of us, taught us things; we went to school there. We were all there for different reasons."

Even after a year, when their mother was back on her feet, she still needed to prove her stability before the girls were returned to her custody.

"My mother worked hard to win us back," Muller added.

Bea Seidl recalled a cold day in 1942 as she was deposited at the St. Joseph's Orphanage with no explanation as to why her mother lost custody of her and her siblings.

"Sister Edythe closed the door, pulled the chair to the room's center and snapped her fingers at me, indicating I was to sit down. I thought otherwise and almost made it to the door before the nun caught me by the arm and

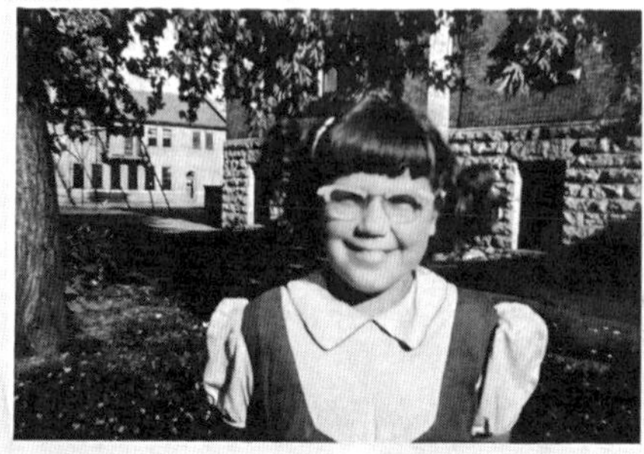
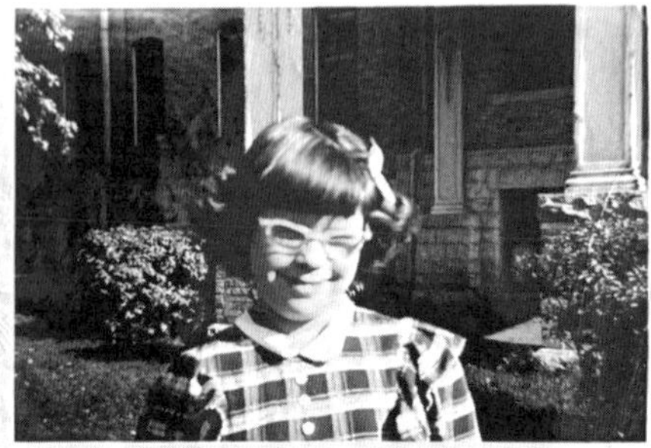

At Christmastime, local groups from Brownie troops to reformatory inmates made sure that no child housed at the orphanage went without a gift. *Muller family photo.*

forced me into the chair. Producing a pair of scissors, she cut my hair with no thought to any style. It fell to the floor in ragged bunches," she recalled in her book *Orphan Doors*.

"Sister Edythe undressed me and tossed my new dress and shoes away as if they were rags. Before I could object, the nun motioned me into a shower where she proceeded to scrub me from head to toes.

"Out of the shower, I sneezed as she raked a powdery substance through what remained of my hair."

Seidl spent eight years with what she described as stern nuns, rigid regimens, and scant tenderness.

But as more and more national reform was instituted and the Depression subsided, the number of institutionalized children declined.

CLOSING THE DOORS

The city rallied around the orphanage, often hosting various benefits throughout its decades-long existence. One of the most significant—and one of the highlights of the local social pages—was started in 1947 by the Nazareth Guild of the St. Joseph's Orphanage.

Each year for more than a decade, the Orphans' Benefit Ball offered local socialites the opportunity to "waltz into the heart of an orphan" at Riverside ballroom. The funds were used to purchase items that could not be obtained by the diocese for the orphanage, such as playground equipment, kitchen equipment, redecorating and updating the facilities, and other large-ticket items needed to serve the children.

The 1954 Orphans' Benefit event was held to buy additional furnishings for the new orphanage residence building.

Due to safety concerns for the children living in the original building, the Catholic Diocese of Green Bay and local parishes funded a new dormitory, which was constructed in 1953 and dedicated in 1954. The building and a new chapel were constructed at a cost of over $600,000. The new dormitory housed eight rooms each for boys and girls. Each room could accommodate eight children apiece.

At Christmastime, local groups from Brownie troops to reformatory inmates made sure that no child housed at the orphanage went without a gift.

In 1955, the Brownie and Scout troops became a part of St. Joseph's Home for Children, as it would soon be called, giving the children an opportunity for further fellowship and learning.

The uniforms for the new recruits were, once again, provided by the Nazareth Guild. However, the orphanage was admitting fewer and fewer children as more and more were placed in foster homes.

In 1957, the home adopted a program targeting teenage girls with "problems" and, two years later, instituted a similar program for boys ages thirteen through eighteen. Placement of the children was handled directly through the court system, and the program dealt primarily with local youth, with some consideration to children coming from other areas of the state.

At that time, Home Director Reverend Eugene Hotchkiss told the *Green Bay Press-Gazette* that "the picture concerning the handling of juvenile[s] has been changing rapidly in recent years, but actually it goes back to 1933 with the adoption of such things as Social Security, Aid to Dependent Children and other means of government financial support."

The boys would now be housed in Don Bosco Hall, while the girls were placed in Madonna Hall.

Another program was started at the home to receive children ages two through fourteen and house them for one month while placing them with an agency.

In 1967, the facility became a boys' home, and two years later, the home began selling the furnishings from unused rooms to help cover expenses.

By 1977, there were just a dozen boys at the facility.

In 1980, the St. Joseph Home for Boys was merged with Our Lady of Charity School Center, and the boys were moved to the Our Lady of Charity grounds, effectively closing the doors to a facility designed to care for area children for nearly nine decades.

Chapter 2

THE HOUSE THAT BROWN COUNTY BUILT

Brown County Veterans Memorial Arena—more commonly referred to as Brown County Arena—was dedicated to the nation's World War II veterans.

The Brown County Board originally planned to divide a $150,000 war memorial fund among the cities of De Pere and Green Bay and the villages of Denmark, Pulaski, and Wrightstown. This was approved by the board in 1945 following the war.

"Each would receive a portion of the $150,000 bond issue according to its population and assessed valuation, with the understanding that county funds would be matched to the extent of 65% by the area," a November 10, 1945 *Press-Gazette* article stated.

"It was indicated that the living memorials would probably be in the form of buildings for public use and that each area's share in its memorial could be spread out over a five-year period."

The following year, the Green Bay City Council unanimously approved the creation of a new city hall and auditorium.

After nearly a decade of studies and talks, it was decided that a multipurpose arena was needed and it should be taken on as a countywide project.

After several more years of planning, the county broke ground on September 22, 1957.

The nearly $2 million, 5,248-seat arena opened in November 1958 on the corner of what was then known as Highland Avenue—now Lombardi

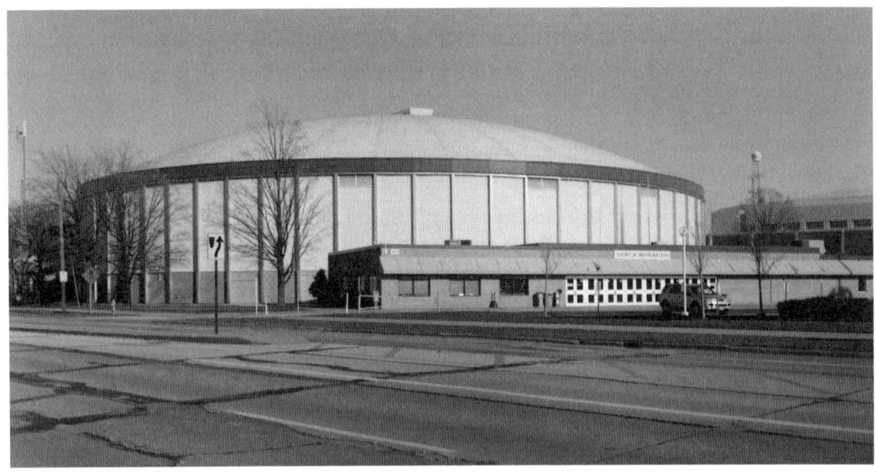

An early photo of the Brown County Arena. *J. Shimon & J. Lindemann photo.*

Avenue—and Oneida Street in Ashwaubenon. It was the first large-capacity entertainment venue in Greater Green Bay during a time when Lambeau Field did not accommodate stadium-size acts. The arena allowed the city to attract more well-known acts to the area and was the only venue to do so until the Resch Center opened in 2002.

In the 1960s, the arena played host to acts such as Gary Lewis and the Playboys, Dobie Gray, Sonny & Cher, Duke Ellington, and the Crystals.

During the 1970s, the arena was a stop for the Association, the Beach Boys, Johnny and June Carter Cash, the Statler Brothers, the Guess Who, Chuck Berry, Muddy Waters, Santana, Loggins & Messina, Ozark Mountain Daredevils, Steppenwolf, Frankie Valli and the Four Seasons, Blue Öyster Cult, REO Speedwagon, Tanya Tucker, Johnny Paycheck, Alice Cooper, Foghat, Linda Ronstadt, Charlie Daniels Band, Aerosmith, Kansas, Styx, Head East, Chicago, Jethro Tull, Cheap Trick, Frank Zappa, ZZ Top, Eric Carmen, the Sweet, Fleetwood Mac, Boston, Heart, KISS, Dolly Parton, Mac Davis, Elvis Presley, Ted Nugent, Charley Pride, Supertramp, Tom Jones, Foreigner, Little River Band, Marty Robbins, Gordon Lightfoot, Doobie Brothers, Van Halen, Journey, Seals & Croft, Barbara Mandrell, Mel Tillis, Kenny Rogers, Dottie West, the Cars, Ted Nugent, Sha-Na-Na, and many more.

The 1980s saw many of the bands from the previous decade return, along with Molly Hatchet, Rush, .38 Special, Marshall Tucker Band, Oak Ridge Boys, Whitesnake, Pure Prairie League, Ozzy Osbourne, Def Leppard, Jefferson Starship, the Greg Kihn Band, Loverboy, Quarterflash,

Black Sabbath, Elvis Costello, Rick Springfield, Air Supply, Van Halen, Pat Benatar, George Jones, Quiet Riot, Judas Priest, Great White, Huey Lewis & the News, Berlin, Quiet Riot, Sammy Hagar, Dokken, Joe Walsh, Sawyer Brown, John Waite, Nitty Gritty Dirt Band, Alabama, Bellamy Brothers, the Monkees, David Lee Roth, Tesla, Stevie Ray Vaughan, Ratt, Poison, Night Ranger, Helix, Megadeth, Scorpions, Lita Ford, Stryper, White Lion, Metallica, Queensrÿche, Cinderella, Reba McEntire, Ricky Van Shelton, Clint Black, and more.

In addition to returning acts, the 1990s ushered in new acts like Mötley Crüe, Faster Pussycat, Slaughter, Warrant, Damn Yankees, Bad Company, Marie Osmond, the Judds, Billy Dean, Skid Row, Soundgarden, Randy Travis, Firehouse, Tesla, Travis Tritt, Steve Miller Band, America, Restless Heart, John Michael Montgomery, Aaron Tippin, Hank Williams Jr., Trisha Yearwood, Little Texas, Confederate Railroad, Barry Manilow, Bob Dylan, Alan Jackson, Billy Ray Cyrus, Crosby Stills & Nash, Kenny G, Brooks & Dunn, Soul Asylum, Vince Gill, Patty Loveless, Boyz II Men, Asleep at the Wheel, Tim McGraw, Blues Traveler, Martina McBride, Jeff Foxworthy, Goo Goo Dolls, BoDeans, and others.

During its last two decades, the arena added Brad Paisley, B.J. Thomas, Trans-Siberian Orchestra, Godsmack, Kenny Chesney, Lee Ann Womack, Toby Keith, Nickelback, Korn, Aaron Carter, Ludacris, Lee Greenwood, All-American Rejects, Blake Shelton, Miranda Lambert, Shinedown, Skillet, Gary Allan, Luke Bryan, Papa Roach, and others to the new acts making a stop there.

The arena also served as home to several sports teams, including the UW–Green Bay basketball teams and the Bobcats hockey team, during its lifetime.

THE PACKERS HALL OF FAME

In July 1976, what was deemed a "million dollar Packer scrapbook" opened in the Brown County Arena.

"[The] facility [is valued] at nearly $1 million and places the value of the exhibits it houses at approximately $300,000. But the sentimental value of irreplaceable items from the Packers' storied past do not have a price tag," Don Langenkamp wrote in the *Press-Gazette*.

The original Packers Hall of Fame—the first of its kind for the National Football League—offered several rooms of team memorabilia. The "Locker

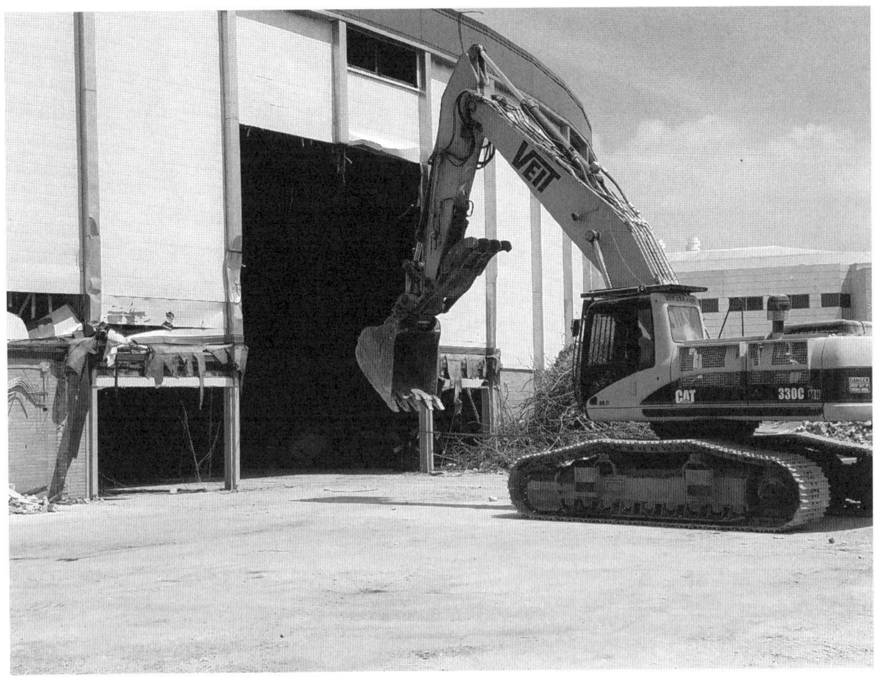

In 2019, the arena was razed to make way for a new $93 million expo center, Resch Expo. *Brown County photo.*

Room" was a two-part area offering reproductions of former players' lockers in one half and a projector showing training room activities in the other. A separate room hosted a mini-theater offering seating for seventy new people every thirty minutes for a Packers history film. The "Playing Field" offered fourteen exhibits of photos, memorabilia, and Packers memories in what was considered the main hall.

In late 1977, work began on a 4,500-square-foot expansion on the arena. The additional room expanded office space as well as the ticket facilities.

A decade later, work began on the Brown County Exposition Hall (later known as Shopko Hall).

A grand opening was held on September 27, 1986, and the facility was billed as "Northeast Wisconsin's Entertainment and Exhibition Showplace," now offering the arena, exposition hall, and Packers Hall of Fame.

In 2019, the arena was razed to make way for a new $93 million expo center, Resch Expo, but not before one last big event.

THE LAST SHOW

On April 6, 2019, Bret Michaels closed down the arena before a sold-out crowd.

Michaels and his band Poison launched three tours at the arena in 1988, 1990, and 1993 and recorded their music video for their hit ballad "Every Rose Has Its Thorn" there as well.

"Bret Michaels was the obvious choice to close the building. The last time he was here with Poison a couple of years ago, he asked for a tour of the arena, he wanted to reminisce. Obviously, he has a lot of history in the building," Terry Charles, from PMI Entertainment Group, told the *Press-Gazette* in 2019.

"We started off every world tour, even some of the solo tours right here in this building," Michaels recalled to the *Press-Gazette*. "Besides it being great memories, it has also brought me great luck.

"The big final night, I wanted to be here for that. One of the most amazing moments in my life is when we shot 'Every Rose Has Its Thorn' video here. It was such a great chemistry....'Every Rose Has Its Thorn' is one of the longest remaining No. 1 songs on the charts, so Green Bay has brought some awesome luck."

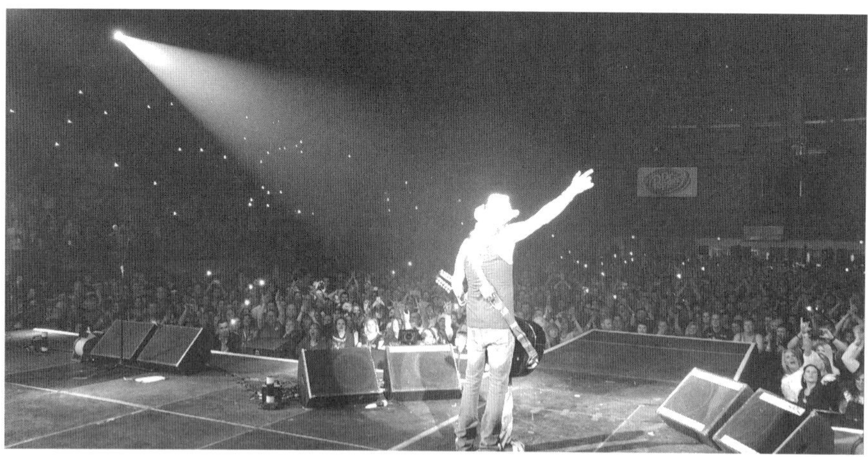

On April 6, 2019, Bret Michaels closed down the arena before a sold-out crowd. *David Gormley photo.*

Chapter 3

A PASSAGEWAY FOR WESTWARD EXPANSION

After the War of 1812, American immigrants settling the country needed to protect their territory from those wishing to claim or reclaim the land and its bounty. As they pushed westward to capture the fur trade, a chain of government forts sprang up in the western Great Lakes region to protect the river routes and the settlers who were staking their claim.

In 1816, Fort Howard was established on the western bank of the Fox River below the bay of Green Bay. The fort linked Fort Niagara in New York and Fort Detroit in Michigan with Fort Winnebago in Portage, Fort Crawford in Prairie du Chien, and Fort Snelling in St. Paul, Minnesota, and became an integral site for trade, due to its location, and a passageway for westward expansion.

A letter from Captain of Rifles John O'Fallon to General Duncan McArthur, dated September 24, 1816, chronicled the selection of the site for the fort. "After looking for some days for a proper site, [Major Charles Gratiot] has finally fixed on the position where the old French fort formerly stood. It will be a stockade with strong pickets, a bastion at each angle, with a piece of artillery on each, amply sufficient to beat off any [Native American] force that can be brought against it," he wrote.

"The fort is situated about one mile up the river and half mile below where commences a mongrel French settlement that extends about five miles on both sides of the river and is occupied by about 40 families."

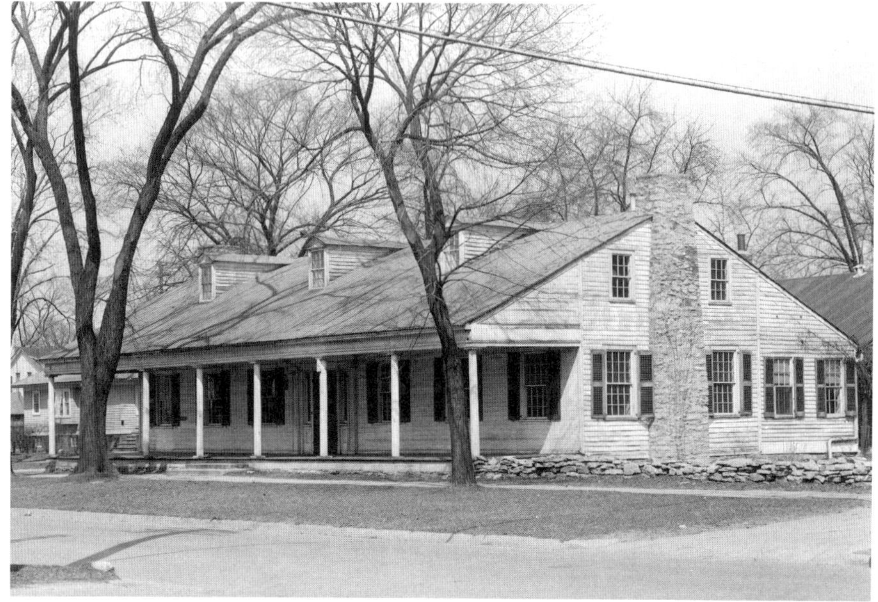

The Fort Howard Hospital structure in 1934. It was relocated to Heritage Hill in 1975. *Library of Congress photo.*

The government allocated $21,000 for the fort's construction, and it was christened Fort Howard in honor of General Benjamin Howard.

By 1819, the personnel at Fort Howard totaled 554 soldiers.

In 1820, H.R. Schoolcraft visited the fort, writing in his journal, "It consists of a range of log barracks, facing three sides of a square parade, and surrounded by a stockade of timber, 30 feet high, with blockhouses at the angles. The whole is whitewashed, and presents a neat military appearance."

When Colonel Joseph Lee Smith assumed command of the fort, he moved it to higher ground—a place that would serve as a better vantage point or lookout.

A stockade was created across the river in 1820 and named Camp Smith on land that is now located inside Heritage Hill State Historical Park.

Green Bay's Heritage Hill remains a keeper of that history, with several preserved buildings and other reconstructions that hold the story of Fort Howard:

FORT HOWARD GUARD HOUSE: Originally built by the U.S. Army in 1833–35 and relocated to Heritage Hill in 2010; it was constructed on the west bank of the Fox River.

Fort Howard Hospital: Originally built by the U.S. Army outside the fort's perimeter; it was relocated to Heritage Hill in 1975. The hospital is listed on the National Register of Historic Places.

Fort Howard Officers' Quarters: A reproduction was built in 1982 at Heritage Hill.

Fort Howard Post School: A reproduction was built in 1982 at Heritage Hill.

Company Kitchen/Orderly Room: The structure was built by the U.S. Army Fifth Infantry Regiment in 1835 and relocated to Heritage Hill. The building is listed on the National Register of Historic Places.

Chapter 4

A FORERUNNER IN GREEN BAY CHILDCARE

The Catholic Woman's Club was formed in the fall of 1900 as an organized society of St. John's Church and then christened with the name "Social Workers." Through 125 years of charitable work and community enrichment, the club celebrated its quasquicentennial club year.

The organization originated at the hands of Mrs. Frank Van Laanen to raise funding for the St. John the Evangelist parish school.

Social Workers club meetings rotated around the homes of club members and focused on the intellectual, social, and charitable work for area youth. In May 1907—the end of the organization's club year—the Social Workers became the Catholic Woman's Club.

"Since the organization in 1900, the work has broadened and the old name had become something of a misnomer, consequently it was decided to adopt a name which would better express the aims of the club," a May 29, 1907 *Press-Gazette* article stated.

The Catholic Woman's Club combined literary and social programs and events with charitable works for those in need and continued to focus on their own literary and cultural enrichment. The women met every Tuesday for nearly six decades.

One of their largest fundraising projects started in 1910 and ran for a decade, collecting new shoes for area schoolchildren. The club even went as far as collecting tinfoil to use for the shoe funds, which in large quantities had a market value at that time. Club members asked area residents to save the foil from gum, candy, cigars, and other items to use for this purpose, stating that "a piece of foil will put a button on a shoe."

In 1913, the organization removed the "Catholic" requirement for membership—focusing more on "good character, intelligence, and general uprightness of conduct"—and its fifty-member limit. The club doubled in size and retained the word "Catholic" in its name.

During the organization's earlier years, prospective members were voted on using black and white balls, with a majority of white balls signaling approval. "People used to think Catholic Woman's Club was for the elite. I don't think anyone was ever turned away, but that was the image [people] had [of the club]. You had to be invited at first but…later on…you could just apply to join," former member Bea Linzmeyer stated in an oral history collected by Eileen Coe.

In 1919, a new group project became synonymous with the club as members began to see that the children of working parents had a need for daycare. Following an eight-month trial term, the Green Bay Day Nursery was made a permanent program in Green Bay.

"The nursery will continue its work in the former quarters in the building at 128 South Monroe Avenue, with greatly increased facilities and with plans for obtaining a larger income for the work," a November 6, 1919 *Press-Gazette* article stated. The facilities were donated by trustees of the cathedral parish.

The following year, the organization purchased the property at 423 East Walnut Street, Green Bay, for use as a clubhouse. A nursery and auditorium were added in the rear of the building.

The Green Bay Day Nursery would later become Encompass Child Care, a forerunner in childcare programs. The club's success was only amplified by the structure that served as its home base.

"The Allouez Community house is one of the finest clubhouses in the state. It is the only institution of its kind that has been erected and will be maintained through the efforts of the Catholic club," an October 14, 1921 *Press Gazette* article stated of the club facilities located on East Walnut Street.

> *Light, airy bedrooms offer a haven for transient women and girls, to those in distress, and permanent homes for a limited number of girls who are working away from home and appreciate a home of beauty and comfort.*
>
> *Mrs. Hubbard, the matron of the nursery, remains to care for the youngsters who moved to new quarters in the community house. The nursery*

ranks with the best in the country and houses an average of 15 children daily, ranging from infants to 10 years of age.

The clubhouse will be supported solely through the activities of the club and the auxiliary and the rents derived from the auditorium, the bedrooms and the house proper.

But after the city levied a tax of $325 on the Allouez Community House property in 1922, the club went to battle against the City of Green Bay, asking the circuit court to enjoin the city and its officials from collecting it. The club was claiming that on the grounds it was a benevolent association without capital stock in which no member benefited financially, it should be exempt from taxation due to nonprofit status. Circuit court judge Henry Graass supported the club's argument.

Unhappy with the loss of that tax revenue over the years of club ownership on that property, the city appealed, and the matter went to the state supreme court. The Wisconsin Supreme Court upheld the ruling.

With the onset of World War II, the club added work with the American Red Cross Blood Bank to its numerous charitable works in the Green Bay community.

In 1950, the club marked its Golden Jubilee year with an extensive redecorating project at 423 East Walnut. "The spacious quarters, tastefully done in pastel green with mulberry carpeting, green satin drapes and solid oak woodwork, includes a reception hall, music room, living room, library and dining room, all on the main floor and all interconnected with wide doorways which are equipped with sliding doors so that any part of the space could be shut off for smaller gatherings," a *Press-Gazette* article stated.

The club also marked its fiftieth year with a mortgage burning—a fitting way to enter its next decade in the community.

In 1954, the Catholic Woman's Club (CWC) introduced the Cabrini book study club, held at the Allouez Community House and scheduled around breakfast. Cabrini later joined with Avila to offer joint breakfast programs at St. Norbert College.

A couple of years later, a garden club was added, named the St. Fiacre Garden Club in recognition of a thirteenth-century Irish monk who is noted as the patron saint of gardeners. The group assisted the wildlife sanctuary and Heritage Hill, along with other charitable works.

In May 1964, the club said goodbye to its longtime clubhouse after the *Green Bay Press-Gazette* purchased it. The newspaper razed the sixty-three-year-old building to expand its facilities on Walnut Street. The club used a portion of the proceeds to fund the Newman Center at 338 Hartung Street. The center was to be used as a resource for Catholic students at UW–Green Bay and as facilities for club activities.

In 1975, the CWC marked its seventy-fifth year, still honoring its commitment to social and philanthropic work in the community.

In 1981, the Newman Center moved to the new UW–Green Bay campus, and the club sold the building to Green Bay Day Nursery. Meetings then moved to the St. John the Evangelist Church, where they remain today.

In 1999, the CWC kicked off a yearlong centennial celebration by presenting a $100,000 check to the Catholic Foundation of the Diocese of Green Bay.

The theme for the 100th year was "Pioneers in Community Giving," reflecting the vision of its original members who filled roles later conducted by social services and other organizations.

"Whether people realize it or not, Catholic Woman's Club paved the way in lay leadership with trendsetting responses to community and social needs. As a result, Catholic Woman's Club has made a mark in the diocese and in Northeast Wisconsin," CWC President Rosemary Hinkfuss said.

Chapter 5

WHEN CITY TRANSPORTATION WENT *CLANG, CLANG, CLANG*

The electric streetcar, or trolley, first appeared in Wisconsin in Appleton in 1886 and slowly worked its way to Fort Howard and Green Bay. The electric trolley system was often a city service, operated by public utilities and sometimes power plants.

In the fall of 1892, the City of Green Bay and its mayor, James H. Almore, were being romanced by several hopefuls who wished to bring streetcar service to the city. Jackson I. Case and Charles H. Holmes, of Racine, were the frontrunners proposing a track on Main Street (from Main and 11th to the other side of the Main Street Bridge close to the Northwestern depot) and on Walnut Street (from the Brown County Fairgrounds to Washington Street) and Washington Street (from Main to Mason Street and across the Mason Street Bridge), as well as a loop servicing Main and Monroe Streets to Porlier, up Webster to Mason.

Some area residents, however, were leery of streetcars, afraid that they would frighten horses and prevent those in the country from traveling into the city. And they had reasons for their concerns, as newspapers recounted incidents such as a February 1899 report of a "horse being driven by Matt Reily on Broadway" that was frightened by a streetcar and ran away. Reily was thrown from his cutter and the cutter smashed.

Citizens and businesspeople with property on Main Street stood up to the council, urging them to relocate the line to Pine Street. The council at first voted down the franchise, but on September 16, 1892, the motion passed.

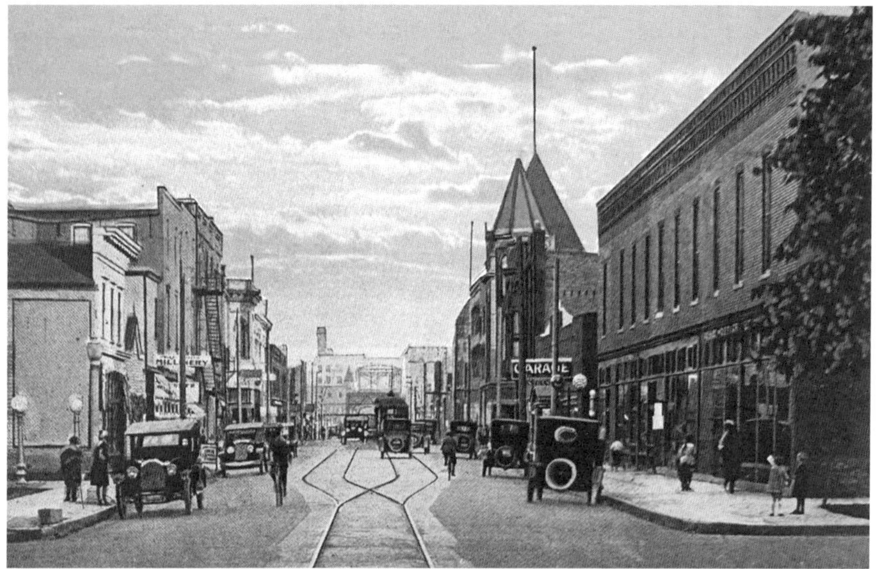

West Walnut Street looking east in Green Bay with a clear view of the trolley tracks. *Green Bay Post Card Company/Darlene & Dick Charneski collection.*

"Its provisions are the same as the one which preceded it. There is no project which has ever aroused greater interest in the city than this one and citizens generally are desirous of seeing it an accomplished fact which the coming season will secure," a *Press-Gazette* article stated.

In the summer of 1893, secondhand cars from Racine were brought north and placed into service.

The operator of the streetcar stood in the front on a platform with little in the way of protection. Passengers entered from the rear and paid their fare in "chits" (six for a quarter) in a box up front. Chits were matched to the number of riders, and if the two didn't line up, the car would sit until it did. Streetcar service ran every hour.

The August 23, 1894 edition of the *Green Bay Weekly Gazette* announced the future arrival of the trolley in Fort Howard as the "Fort Howard Shake," with local businessmen and legislators championing the cause at the city's common council meeting the week before.

Those speaking at the council meeting scheduled to present the ordinance to create the trolley system saw it as "another bond drawing Fort Howard and Green Bay closer together and prove a strong factor in bringing about annexation of the two cities, a thing much desired by many people in both cities," the article stated. The ordinance passed, with just one alder opposing.

The franchise was granted to Fort Howard banker David McCartney, who was also seeking an electric-light plant franchise at the time. The ordinance provided that the construction of the road start in ninety days for a franchise term lasting twenty-five years.

In 1899, the two lines became one, and Fox River Valley Electric Railway began handling transportation operations in Green Bay and Fort Howard. That same year, vestibules were added to the cars to protect the operators.

In 1899, a railway was constructed to De Pere, followed by Duck Creek in 1902 and Kaukauna in 1903. The Brown County Historical Society said that a building was constructed on South Washington Street to house the trolley cars for the De Pere line.

"In later years, the building served as the transit garage for the city buses. While the original facade had been partially obscured by several additions and alterations, the building still retained its distinctive exterior cornice and its impressive timber roof trusses. With the construction of the new bus terminal and garage on University Avenue, the old car barn was demolished in 2002," the society noted.

"Trolley parties" became a thing in the Green Bay area, favored especially by women's groups, as they took to open cars for their gatherings. The streetcar company later created special lighted cars for the sole purpose of accommodating these groups.

On November 17, 1937, the city officially said farewell to the streetcar after four decades of service. Thousands filled the streets as a half-mile-long parade moved down city streets to commemorate the "honorable discharge" of the trolleys.

During the celebration, Association of Commerce President J.M. Conway recalled the beginning of trolley service forty-three years earlier. "When this city's streets were paved with cedar blocks and brick, and the main industry was lumber manufacture, we looked down the river to Appleton where they had a contraption that hauled people around with an electric motor," he said. "Chicago still had the wondrous horse-drawn vehicles. But we looked to Appleton, and all the arguments that were put forth didn't prevent Green Bay from getting in line."

The following morning, twelve new Wisconsin Public Service "streetliners," or buses, moved down Washington and Walnut Streets, making their inaugural run in the city.

Chapter 6

THE TRAGIC STORY OF THE LOST DAUPHIN

On a hill along the Fox River just south of Green Bay sits a park. The park is a quiet, peaceful place with little but history to show what once existed there and how it may or may not have been tied to a kingdom in France.

In March 1785, a son was born to King Louis XVI and Marie Antoinette as a royal banner waved high in the air announcing the new arrival. The baby grew into a young boy enjoying a gay and privileged life. When his older brother, Louis Joseph, died in June 1789, Louis Charles became dauphin—the oldest son of the king of France and heir to the throne.

In August 1789, the National Constituent Assembly voted to abolish the feudal system, and the French Revolution broke out. In August 1792, the family's palace was stormed, and they were imprisoned days later at "the temple." After King Louis XVI and Marie Antoinette faced the guillotine, a man named Antoine Simon was assigned to care for the ten-year-old boy by the Committee of Public Safety.

The boy's story found its way around the globe and to America. An article in a February 1853 issue of *Putnam's Monthly Magazine*, written by a clergyman, John H. Hanson, stated:

> *The sad history of this child, his beauty, his virtues and his sufferings are familiar to all.*
>
> *After separation from his female relatives and the death of his mother in 1793, he was consigned to the care of Simon the cobbler. By him, he*

> *was treated in a manner which disgraces humanity: cold, hunger, filth, sleeplessness, beating, abuse, terror.*

After the fall of Maximilien Robespierre—a key figure in the French Revolution—and the execution of Simon, Louis Charles's suffering was alleviated. "The existence of Louis XVII was a sore trial for the republicans, who at the same time could frame no excuse, even to themselves, for putting him to death," Hanson wrote.

"In Dec. 1794, a decree was passed in the Convention 'that the committee of government should devise the means of sending the son of Louis out of the territories of the republic.'"

On June 9, 1795, it was reported to the convention that Louis Charles was dead.

"Now, did Louis XVII really die in 1795 as was reported at the time and generally believed since," Hanson wrote, or was he still alive?

Could the story have been so tragic that no one was willing to believe it, or were others just looking for an opportunity? Either way, rumors swirled about the young boy being smuggled out of the situation. All over France, many claimed to be the missing dauphin—the dauphin of Vitry, the dauphin of St. Malo, and as many as five other young boys. But one of the most convincing stories would surface in Green Bay.

A CHANCE MEETING

In February 1853, *Putnam's Magazine* ran the first installment of the story "Have We a Bourbon in Our Midst?" The House of Bourbon—a noble family that ruled France from 1589 to 1792 and 1814 to 1848—descended from Louis I, including the Lost Dauphin. An introduction by Reverend Dr. Hawks provides credibility to the story and to the man claiming to be a part of French royalty: Eleazer Williams.

Reverend John H. Hanson, who relayed the story's 1853 narrative, wrote:

> *I observed about two years ago, a paragraph in the papers, stating that facts had recently come to light which rendered it probably that the Rev. Mr. Williams, of Green Bay, Wisconsin, was none other than Louis XVII, but as the circumstances on which the statement was based were not mentioned, except that he bore a strong resemblance to the Bourbon family, my curiosity*

> *was excited, and I made fruitless inquiries in many quarters, finding no one who could give me the slightest clue to the mystery.*

Then fate stepped in as Williams returned to New York and Hanson had a chance encounter with him on a train there.

Introducing himself as a fellow clergyman, "I told him that I had seen a statement in the newspapers, which had excited my curiousity, and should feel obliged, if it was not intrusive, by being informed if he believed the story of this royal origin, and upon what evidence the extraordinary claim was based," Hanson said.

"He replied that the subject was painful to him, nor could he speak unmoved, but that he would with pleasure give me the required information."

Hanson then asked Williams if he had any memory of Paris or the voyage to the new country.

"Therein, lies the mystery of my life. Everything that occurred to me is blotted out, entirely erased, irrecoverably gone. My mind is blank until 13 or 14 years of age," Williams told Hanson.

Williams said the loss came from diving off a "high rock" into Lake George with a group of Native American boys with whom he resided.

"I was always under the impression," he said, "that I was at least partly of Indian extraction, until the time that the Prince de Joinville came to the country. "

The Prince of Joinville was the third son of Louis Philippe, who was then the French king, whose trip the article claims was to obtain a renunciation to France's throne.

"One of the first questions that he asked on his arrival in New York was whether there was such a person known as Eleazer Williams among the Indians in the northern part of the state; and after some inquiries in different quarters, he was told that there was such a person who was at that time a missionary of the Protestant Episcopal Church at Green Bay," Williams said.

AN INTERVIEW WITH A PRINCE

In an 1853 *Putnam's Magazine* article, Hanson continued to recount Eleazer Williams's tale, as the Prince of Joinville connected with him through the church and asked for an interview with Williams before he returned to France.

"Some time elapsed, and I heard nothing more on the subject, which was beginning to fade from my mind; when one day, while on board a steamer on Lake Michigan, I had an interview with the Prince, who shortly after, at Green Bay, revealed the secret of my birth," Williams said.

> *My reputed mother is still living at a very advanced age. She is now at Caughnawaga* [New York].
>
> *I ought, as soon as the Prince told me the secret of my birth, to have returned to the East and seen her. But I unfortunately neglected to do so for some time, and when I did come, I found that the Romish Priests had been tampering with her, and that her mouth was hermetically sealed.*

Williams claimed that the priests told her, "Suppose that this man should prove to be heir to a throne on the other side of the Great Salt Lake, what injury may he not do to the church. He has been brought up a Protestant, and if he obtained sovereign power it would be the ruin of many souls. You must therefore say nothing one way."

Williams said:

> *But we have had the Baptismal register at Caughnawaga examined, and the priest was made to certify to it, and though the names of all the rest of her children are recorded there, together with the dates of their birth and baptism, mine does not occur there and the births of the children follow so closely upon each other at regular intervals—of two years between each—that it does not seem naturally possible I could have been her child, unless I was a twin to some other child whose birth and baptism are recorded while mine are not.*

Williams also added the story of a French gentleman who died in New Orleans in 1848 with the last name of Belanger "who confessed on his death-bed that he was the person who brought the Dauphin to this country, and placed him among the Indians, in the northern part of the State of New-York."

"It seems that Belanger had taken a solemn oath of secrecy, alike for the preservation of the Dauphin, and the safety of those who were instrumental in effecting his escape, but the near approach of death and the altered circumstances of the times, induced him to break silence before his departure from the world."

On the steamship, Williams also produced a silk dress with about a dozen feet of train. "It is a dress of Marie Antoinette. It was given to me by a person who bought it in France, and who hearing my story, and considering me the rightful owner, made me a present of it."

A NOBLE-LOOKING MAN

Hanson wrote:

> *I now proceeded to scrutinize more closely the form, features and general appearance of Mr. Williams, and to reexamine the scars on his face. He is an intelligent, noble-looking old man.…He speaks correctly and even eloquently as far as style is concerned.…He has the port and presence of a European gentleman of high rank; a nameless something which I never saw but in persons accustomed to command; a countenance bronzed by exposure below the eyebrows; a fair, high, ample, intellectual but receding forehead; a slightly aquiline but rather small nose; a long Austrian lip, the expression of which is of exceeding sweetness when in repose.…*
>
> *I asked him if he could account for the conduct of the Prince de Joinville in disclosing so important a secret as that of his royal birth, and requesting him to give up rights previously unknown to him, and which without information derived from the Prince he would have had no means of ascertaining.*
>
> *However I may add that at this interview Mr. Williams positively declined stating all that passed between him and the Prince de Joinville.*

"My story is on the winds of heaven, and will work its way without me. They have got it in France. Copies of my daguerreotype have been sent to eminent men there," Williams said.

The daguerreotype was the first widely used form of photography used in the 1840s and 1850s, and one such image produced a significant photo of a cross. "The cross represented in the engraving was among the coins and other articles referred to hereafter as having been left with the child. The engraving scarcely does justice to Mr. Williams, or brings out the resemblance to the Bourbons," *Putnam's Magazine* noted.

Hanson noted:

On arriving in New York, I made inquiries concerning the ecclesiastical standing of Mr. Williams, and found that there was a difficulty of determining to what jurisdiction he belonged, resulting from his having been sent out as a missionary to Green Bay....Distance and the lapse of time made the authorities of New York unwilling to recognize him as one of the clergy of this Diocese.

By those who have hitherto paid attention to this mysterious subject, it has been supposed that the young Prince was smuggled into this country by his friends, and hidden away among the Indians to conceal him from the Jacobins.

Those familiar with Williams and his family testified to the fact that his looks were not Native American or similar to the rest of his family but more English or French.

"I may add, they all died of consumption," Hanson wrote. "I found that the fact of the absence of his name from the baptismal register, at Caughnawaga, is undoubted. Mr. Williams has a certified copy from the record at Green Bay."

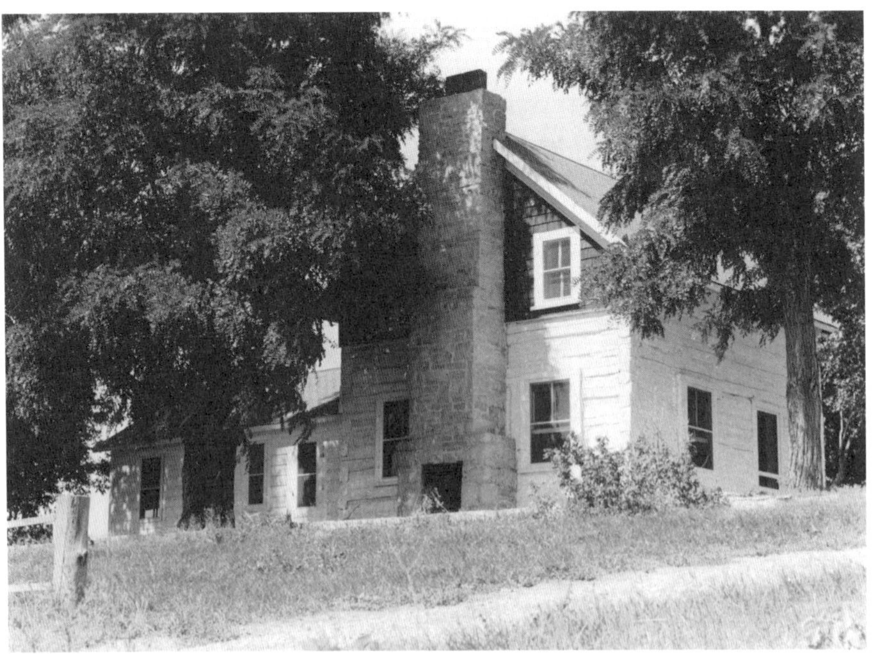

An 1885 photo of Eleazer Williams's log cabin overlooking the Fox River in De Pere. *Wisconsin Conservation Department photo.*

This was explained by the fact that Williams was privately baptized on account of sickness, "which certainly is no reason why his baptism should not have been registered," Hanson added.

A STRONG CASE

Hanson also relays a conversation that Eleazer Williams said took place between the Prince of Joinville and Williams in Green Bay at the Astor Hotel.

The prince told Williams:

> *You have been accustomed, sir, to consider yourself a native of this country, but you are not. You are of foreign descent; you were born in Europe, sir, and however incredible it may at first seem to you, I have to tell you that you are the son of a king.*
>
> *There ought to be much consolation to you to know this fact. You have suffered a great deal, and have been brought very low, but you have not suffered more, or been more degraded than my father, who was long in exile and poverty in this country; but there is this difference between him and you, that he was all along aware of his high birth, whereas you have been spared the knowledge of your origin.*

The prince then produced a piece of parchment paper that contained verbiage that would serve as Williams's renouncing of his right to the throne if signed. Williams conveyed that signing the document "might be the personal consequences to myself, I felt that I could not be the instrument of bartering away with my own hand the rights pertaining to me by my birth, and sacrificing the interests of my family, and that I could only give to him the answer which de Provence gave to the ambassador of Napoleon at Warsaw, 'Though I am in poverty and exile I will not sacrifice my honor.'"

> *The Prince upon this assumed a loud tone, and accused me of ingratitude in trampling on the overtures of the King, his father, who he said was actuated in making the proposition more by feelings of kindness and pity towards me than by any other consideration, since his claim to the French throne rested on an entirely different basis to mine—not that of hereditary descent, but of popular election.*

The *Putnam's Magazine* article goes on to list two dozen points that provide a solid case for Williams and his link to King Louis XVI; these include his likeness to the royal family, various marks on his body that corresponded with those known to have been on the body of the Dauphin, and two boxes of clothing and medals of Louis XVI and Marie Antoinette that were said to have been left with him in his youth.

While the article provided a strong case for Williams, someone would soon come forward to dispute his claims.

CONTROVERSY SPRINGS

When the February 1853 edition of *Putnam's Magazine* reached England, the Prince of Joinville had his secretary write to the London agent for the magazine claiming the story a falsehood.

Aug. Trognon, former preceptor and secretary for the Prince de Joinville, wrote:

> *His first thought was to treat* [it] *with the indifference which it deserves, the absurd invention on which this article is founded, but on reflecting that a little truth is there mixed with much falsehood, the Prince deemed it right that I should in his name give a few lines in reply to show the exact portion of truth there is in this mass of fables.*
>
> *It is very true that in a voyage which he made to the United States towards the end of the year 1841, the Prince finding himself at Machinac met on board the steamboat a passenger whose face he thinks he recognizes in the portrait given in the Monthly Magazine, but whose name had entirely escaped him.*

According to the prince, Eleazer Williams was knowledgeable in North American history and had an Iroquois mother and a French father and was therefore able to regale the prince with stories, as the prince was traveling the area to retrace the path of the French as they established residency in the country.

"Since then, some letters have been exchanged between Mr. Williams and the persons attached to the Prince," he added.

> *But there ends all which the article contains of truth, concerning the relations of the Prince with Mr. Williams. All the rest, all which treats of*

> *the revolution which the Prince made to Mr. Williams of the mystery of his birth, all which concerns the pretended personage of Louis XVII is from one end to the other a work of the imagination—a fable women wholesale, a speculation upon the public credulity.*
>
> *If by chance any of the readers of the monthly magazine should be disposed to avow belief in it, thy should procure from Paris a book which has been very recently published by M. Beauchense. They will there find concerning the life and death of the unfortunate Dauphine, the most circumstantial and positive details.*

From there, controversy erupted in the country for those for and against the likelihood that Williams was the Lost Dauphin. Stories and lectures on both sides hit print mediums and venues, and people even took to traveling to seek out the truth about the Lost Dauphin.

THE DEERFIELD MASSACRE

One of the theories for those seeking the truth about the Lost Dauphin centered on the Deerfield Massacre, which occurred during Queen Anne's War in 1704.

"On the morning of March 1, 1704, just after daybreak, Major Hertel de Rouville, with 200 French and 140 Indians, surprised the sleeping settlement, killing 47 of the inhabitants and making prisoners of 112. Every building in the village, except two, was burned to the ground," recalled the *Boston Evening Transcript* in June 1890.

Some of the Deerfield residents were carried away, including the minister, John Williams, and his wife and some of their children. On their trek through Vermont, newspaper accounts say that Williams's wife collapsed with exhaustion and was put to death on the spot.

While those individuals who were held captive returned to Deerfield in two years, one of the children, Eunice, stayed with the tribe and married a Native American man.

"He was proud of his White wife, took her name and then founded the family which Eleazer Williams belonged by descent," some claimed, which was relayed in a 1923 *Green Bay Press-Gazette* article.

"Thomas Williams, grandson of Eunice, served in the Revolutionary War and was made 'war chief' by the British," the article said, adding that once

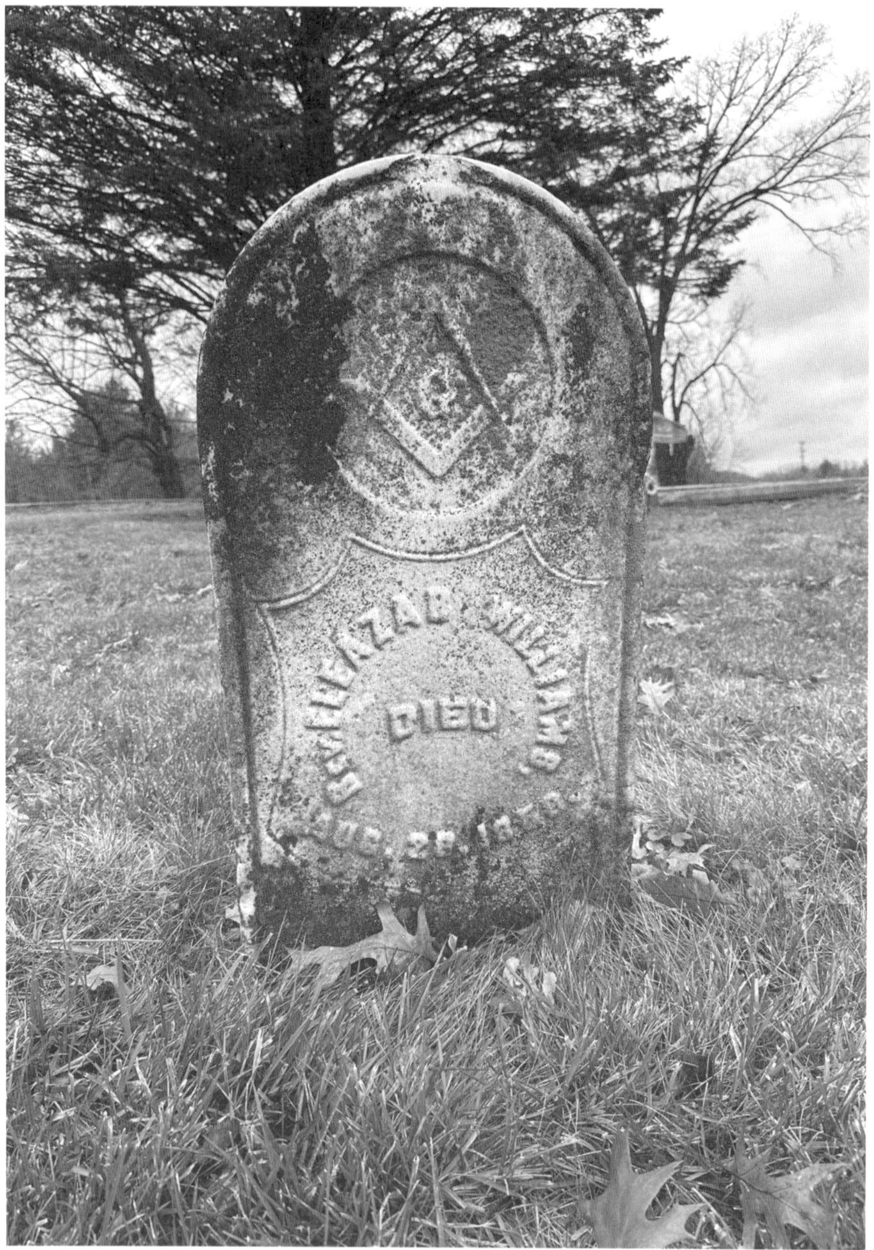

In 1947, Williams's remains and tombstone were moved to the Holy Apostles Church Cemetery at Oneida. *Author photo.*

the war ended, Thomas sought out his white relatives, who proposed that a couple of Thomas's children live with them, receive an education, and return to the tribe as missionaries.

"The next fall, two lads came to live in the deacon's home and to attend school. In the [tribe] the older boy had been called 'Lazau,' but in the deacon's home he was to answer to the dignified name of 'Eleazer' and he was to learn that he took the name from Eleazer Mather, the grandfather of the little girl who had elected to remain with [the tribe]," the article added.

Eleazer attended Dartmouth College and later Hanover before serving in the War of 1812.

"Shortly after the war, he was received into the Episcopal Church and nominated a missionary to the Oneida," the article added.

During the Revolutionary War, the Oneida assisted the new European colonies, serving in General George Washington's army.

In return, the 1794 Treaty of Canandaigua promised the protection of their homelands, stating that the

> *lands reserved to the Oneida, Onondaga, and Cayuga Nations in their respective treaties with the State of New York, and called their reservations, to be their property; and the United States will never claim the same, nor disturb them, or either of the Six Nations, nor their Indian friends, residing thereon, and united with them in the free use and enjoyment thereof; but the said reservations shall remain theirs until they choose to sell the same to the people of the United States, who have the right to purchase.*

A year earlier, the United States had also adopted the Non-Intercourse Act, which prohibited the purchase of Native lands without the government's approval. But the State of New York continued to enter into land transactions, and the Oneida were down to thirty-two acres by the early 1800s. In 1822, the Oneida signed a treaty with the Menominee and Ho-Chunk Nations, purchasing millions of acres as their new homeland.

"The game, land and seasons were familiar in Wisconsin and our people were decidedly more comfortable here. We negotiated with the Menominee to share their lands, and we came to an agreement in 1822," said former general manager/strategist Bill Gollnick during a presentation for the nation's bicentennial celebration.

An article in the Oneida Nation's *Kalihwisaks* read:

> *In 1823, some Oneida families, "First Christian Party" loaded horse-drawn wagons packed up with pine boxes of essentials and what they could carry in a sack and left their homelands. For roughly three weeks they traveled over rough trails to get to the port of Buffalo, N.Y. From there they boarded a ship that took between five to seven days to travel along the western shore of Michigan, through the Mackinaw Island straits then on to Fort Howard in Green Bay. The new territory was the edge of the west and there were no log homes or cleared land, so the Oneidas settled in Little Kakalin on the Fox River roughly 29 miles south.*

"Mr. Williams was a dark-complexioned, good-looking man. Having always heard him spoken of, by his relations in Connecticut, as 'our Indian cousin,' it never occurred to me to doubt his belonging to that race, although I now think that if I had met him elsewhere I should have taken him for a Spaniard or a Mexican," Juliette Magill Kinzie wrote in her 1873 book *Wau-Bun, the Early Day in the Northwest.*

A Legend Endures

According to the biography connected with the Eleazer Williams papers at the Wisconsin Historical Society, shortly after his move to Green Bay, Williams became "negligent in his duties as teacher and missionary" and lost the confidence of the people he was serving.

"He established a school in the area, but its pupils were the children of new white settlers and the few remaining French traders," the biography said.

"In 1823, he married one of his students, Madeline Jourdaine, a Menominee of mixed Indian and French ancestry, who took the name Mary Hobart." The couple built a cabin on the bank of the Fox River, but when the De Pere dam was constructed, they were forced uphill.

Today, Lost Dauphin Park, located south of Green Bay, is situated on nineteen acres of the Williams homestead on land owned by the state since 1947. The land was gifted to the state that year by property owner L.W. Gillespie, on the condition that it be maintained as a state park.

The home on the property was later destroyed by fire.

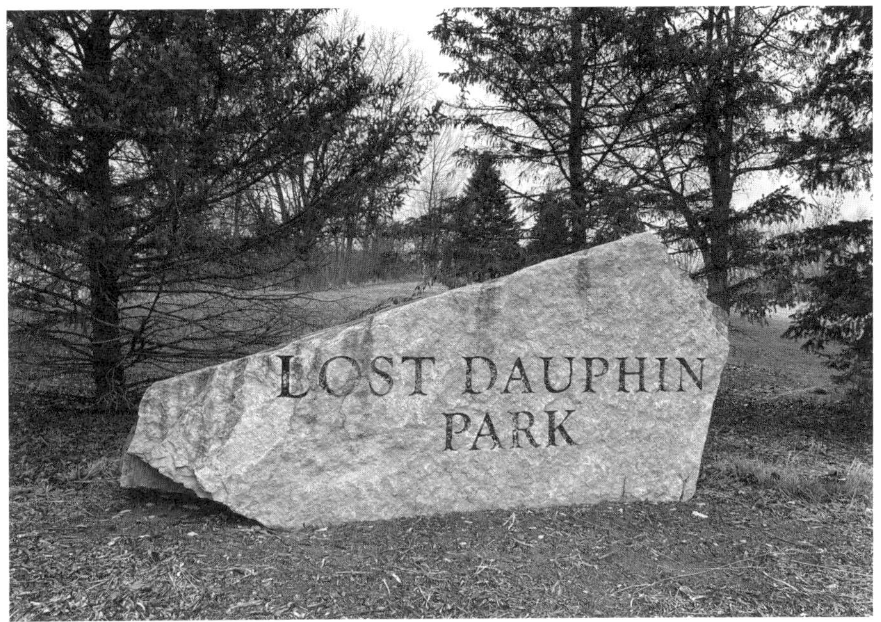

A boulder marking the site of the Lost Dauphin property today. The site now serves as a local park. *Author photo.*

The biography added:

> *By 1832, a council of the Oneida Indians formally repudiated Williams and, upon their request, the church withdrew from him all confidence and support. Williams continued to pursue his plan for an Indian empire in Wisconsin until 1836 when the conclusion of the Schermerhorn Treaty stipulated that the land in the area would be opened to white settlement. Most of the Menominee lands were ceded to the government and the New York Indians were restricted to two small tracts of land.*
>
> *In 1842, Bishop Jackson Kemper censured Williams and requested him to leave the Oneida Indians to their own devices. Following the final demise of his scheme, Williams moved to a small cabin at Kaukauna and spent most of his time traveling on the Great Lakes and along the Eastern Seaboard.*

In 1858, Williams is said to have died poor in New York and was buried there.

In 1947, his remains and tombstone were moved to the Holy Apostles Church Cemetery at Oneida. More than two decades ago, French historians announced that DNA testing from a "preserved heart" of the boy who died in the Paris prison two centuries earlier proved that the boy was in fact the son of King Louis XVI and Marie Antoinette.

The announcement scientifically discredited the claims of Eleazer Williams, but the legend will endure, giving Williams the notoriety he appeared to pursue.

Chapter 7

A FAST-PACED WORLD MARKS THE BEGINNING AND END OF HENRY'S HAMBURGERS

When automobiles became mainstream in America, drive-in restaurants began popping up all over the country as the fast-food industry began catering to an increasingly fast-paced world.

Hoping to cash in on the new industry, the Bresler's Ice Cream Company introduced the first Henry's Hamburgers—named for one of the founders—in the 1950s in Chicago. By the early 1960s, there were more than two hundred Henry's franchise locations across the country—about the same amount that McDonald's had at that time.

In December 1960, the national chain ran an ad in the *Green Bay Press-Gazette* seeking "men interested in owning and operating their own Henry's Drive-ins, which is affiliated with the fastest growing self-service restaurant chain in America, now operating in 29 states and Canadian provinces." The ad requested an investment of $16,000 and one year's rent to begin the franchise.

A "now open" ad ran in the June 7, 1961 edition of the *Press-Gazette* announcing the new location of Henry's Hamburgers on South Main Boulevard at Abrams Street, next to the Hills Brothers Shell Service station. The ad promoted fifteen-cent hamburgers made of 100 percent beef, a twenty-nine-cent fish sandwich, ten-cent French fries, and other menu items.

One week later, the publication said that the franchise location had already sold 14,261 hamburgers.

With the drive-in restaurant also came a "new sensation" called the California Burger, featuring Henry's sauce, pickle, onion, tomato, and

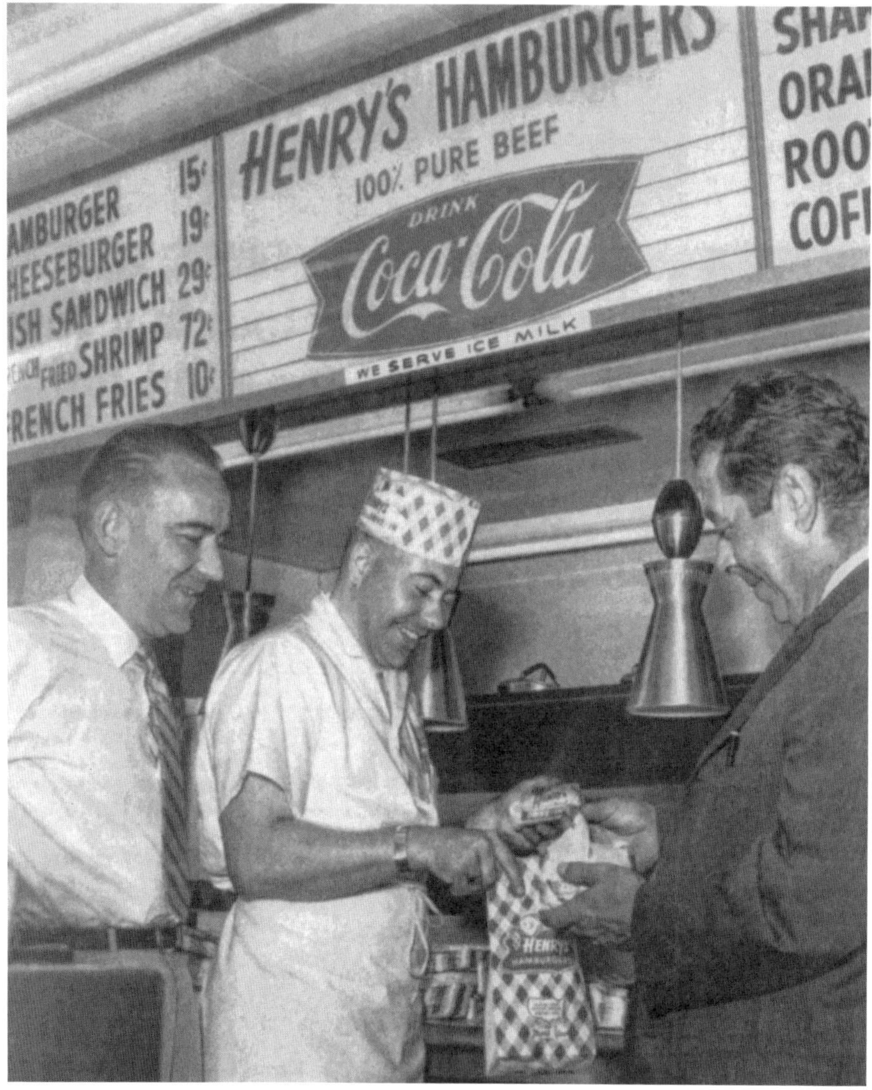

The restaurant enjoyed a little over a decade catering to Green Bay's east side, but while existing restaurants began to make their move to a drive-through setup, Henry's never made the transition. Press-Gazette *photo*.

lettuce—a "meal in a bun." Ads for the business later promoted the hamburgers as ten for one dollar.

The restaurant enjoyed a little over a decade catering to Green Bay's east side, but while existing restaurants began to make their move to a drive-through setup, Henry's never made the transition.

In the 1970s, franchise locations across the country began closing as the Bresler Company began making organizational changes. The last advertisement for the Green Bay location ran in September 1972. The Bresler's ice cream shops, with thirty-three flavors, continued on with 370 outlets nationwide.

In 1987, the Bresler's chain was sold to Oberweis Dairy of Aurora, Illinois, and became the Bresler's division of Oberweis Dairy. The only remaining Henry's Hamburgers today is located in Benton Harbor, Michigan.

"They established a reputation for service and value, listening to their customers instead of the franchisor, which enabled them to remain in business after the Henry's chain ceased to be a player in the 1970s. This was strictly a carryout business until the addition of drive thru service in 1988, which now accounts for over 70% of sales," a history for the remaining franchise stated.

The property that was once home to the Henry's Hamburgers location can be found at 1696 Main Street in Green Bay.

Chapter 8

RETIRED FROM THE WORLD

"For many, many years, ever since it was established in 1882, there has been an atmosphere of mystery connected with the Monastery of Our Lady of Charity of Refuge, or the 'Good Shepherd Home,' as it is commonly but erroneously called," Kate McGuire wrote in a December 1941 edition of the *Press-Gazette*.

> *It is as if those high, gray walls that surround the one-block area held a strange, forbidding secret for many citizens of Green Bay.*
>
> *Many stories, both good and bad, have been whispered about concerning the place; stories with no just cause and with very little truth behind them.*

The reason for the perceived secrecy—the facility was a "cloistered" convent, a home for nuns living in seclusion from the outside world, devoted to prayer and acts of charity.

The Sisters of Our Lady of Charity was an order formed in the seventeenth century in France in dedication to the care, rehabilitation, and education of girls and young women in difficult situations or experiencing homelessness. The Sisters of Our Lady of Charity of the Good Shepherd was formed in 1835, when a new governing structure was created. Seven years later, five sisters were sent to the United States to establish houses.

After they established residency in a four-bedroom home at the intersection of Madison and Milwaukee Streets in Green Bay in 1882, newspaper accounts told the story of challenge, as the order struggled to provide basic necessities. But in time, they were doing well and able to take women and girls into their community; the number of young girls living at the convent reached fifteen in 1885 and 1886.

In 1896, the sisters sold the three-lot property facing St. John's Park to the Sisters of St. Joseph, as their new convent was being completed on Webster Avenue and Porlier Street across from St. Vincent's Hospital.

With no reformatory in the state of Wisconsin for women and girls, there was no institution in which to place convicted females, except the local jail or Waupun prison, so some women were sentenced to the Good Shepherd Home.

In 1914, the Wisconsin State Board of Control sent an inspector to the facility. "The large modern building is surrounded by a high stone wall. It is one of the finest institutions I have visited," the inspector reported. "There are about 150 pupils. These pupils are well taken care of, and are taught music, housekeeping and are given an eighth-grade education."

That same year, a new chapel on the property was dedicated by Bishop Joseph J. Fox.

The sisters not only gave refuge to young "wayward" girls but also became home to women over eighteen who wanted to "retire from the world" and labor and pray at the convent; they were called the Magdalenes.

The convent was dependent on a thriving laundry business to provide for the three groups of residents in the facility. The institution later became known as the Our Lady of Charity School for Girls.

In February 1957, the Our Lady of Charity Guild was organized to work alongside the sisters and aid in fundraising for a new facility. The sisters broke ground in December 1961 on a $2 million facility on a forty-three-acre tract of land on the west side. The facility opened at 2640 West Point Road in 1963 and, by 1968, included a gymnasium and indoor pool.

The Porlier property was sold to St. Vincent's, which had constructed a new hospital facility, and the building was razed shortly after.

Chapter 9

THE PASSING OF THE PACKERS' NAME

"The story about the company is just fascinating history," said Green Bay Packers historian Cliff Christl. Christl completed extensive research on the Acme Packing Company's story while compiling Green Bay Packers' history for publication in projects such as the four-volume book set *The Greatest Story in Sports* and the *Packers Heritage Trail* book. "I probably enjoyed researching that as much as anything else in the book, that and Prohibition's effect on the Packers," Christl stated.

But the story begins with Indian Packing, which was once located on Morrow Street between Elizabeth and Henry Streets in Green Bay. The company came to Green Bay in 1916 through a joint plant project with the Green Bay Stockyards & Transit Company, Green Bay Packing Company, and what was then known as Indian Packing Company. The project was deemed "the most important project ever undertaken for the city" at the time by the *Green Bay Press-Gazette*.

Construction plans called for four fireproof buildings, with the largest being a four-story packinghouse in proximity to the Northwestern Railroad and Green Bay & Western and accessible through switch by the St. Paul Railway. The grounds would also include stock sheds, pens, yards, and an office able to handle one thousand heads of stock—beef, hogs, sheep, and calves—per day, which were never used.

The Indian Packing Company was organized in the city that year with $100,000 in capital stock, with existing operations in Pennsylvania and Rhode Island.

"The establishment of the Indian Packing company gives the Green Bay Packing company the unusual advantage of starting in business with an established concern that has a growing trade and an established selling force on the road to handle all of the products," a March 1917 *Press-Gazette* article stated.

During World War I, the Green Bay meatpacking industry was doing well as cattle for feeding American troops was shipped to Chicago and Green Bay for processing. The new U.S. Food Administration (now FDA) was urging families to aid in the war effort by saving meat consumption for the war effort with "Meatless Monday" and other campaigns.

The rise in meat production and Indian Packing's success showed in their contributions to the Green Bay area, including sponsoring a baseball team, bowling team, and fledgling football squad. Plans for the football team were being made in August 1919, as the Indian Packing Corporation was announcing concepts for extensive additions to the Green Bay plant, following the acquisition of Green Bay Packing and the New England Supply Company in Rhode Island.

Meanwhile, Indian Packing stock was dropping from $44.50 to $39.50 to $38.50 after being placed on the Curb Market at the end of July.

The Indian Packing team held their second organizational meeting on August 14, 1919, which was chronicled in a *Press-Gazette* article that stated, "Indications point to the Indians having the greatest team in the history of football in Green Bay and there is no doubt but that the gridiron fans will see a great exhibition of pigskin chasing at Hagemeister Park this fall."

Curly "Earl" Lambeau was selected as captain, and the first game was set for September 14.

The first Packers team photo was shot in front of the Indian Packing plant's long garage structure, and practices were held on the plant grounds in 1919; that building and many other structures have since been razed.

By their first game, Indian Packing stock had dropped to $26.50 and later fell to $19.00.

Christl explained:

> *I knew that they sold stock, but I knew nothing about what was called the Curb Market.... The Curb Market was an outdoor market in New York, on Broad Street in front of—I think—the Wall Street Journal building, where they sold stock on the windows, second-story windows, and that's how Acme and Indian stock was sold; it wasn't on the New York Stock*

> *Exchange. So, as a result, there were a lot of shysters involved in the process. And I think that has led to some of their financial issues.*

In December 1920, the Acme Packing Company of Chicago announced its plans to purchase the Indian Packing Company. By that time, stock had dropped to $3.25.

The company took over the plant and the name of the baseball and football teams in 1921—the same year that the football team was admitted into the American Professional Football Association (now the National Football League) as the Acme Packers.

By the end of 1921, Acme Packing was $3.65 million in debt, and in January 1922, new officers were elected during the company's annual meeting, hoping to turn the finances around. By that time, the Packers had moved their practices to Hagemeister Park, and the Acme name was slowly slipping from its attachment to the team.

According to Christl, a late 1921 publication of "The Dope Sheet: Official Program and Publication, Acme-Packers Football Team" noted:

> *The Acme Packing Company does not own nor financially back the Packer team. The team is owned and managed and is financially backed by Messrs. J. Emmett and John Clair of the Acme Packing Corp.*
>
> *The Acme Packing Company equipped the team and started it out with uniforms bearing their names but the interest in the team aside from this is none other than that of a progressive Green Bay plant wishing to see a Green Bay team clean up the country.*

It also stated that "the Clair brothers at the offset of the season agreed to be financially responsible and the younger Mr. Clair assumed the active management of the club."

The rights were later surrendered back to the team that became the Green Bay Packers.

Chapter 10

THE RISE AND FALL OF THE PORT PLAZA MALL

The development of the downtown shopping mall began decades before any land was moved for the Port Plaza mall in Green Bay—all the way back to 1956 and the creation of the Gregby Committee. Gregby—a contraction of Greater Green Bay—hired a Los Angeles firm to draw a master plan for a shopping center. After years of trial and error, in February 1967, the council approved three resolutions that would adopt a Gregby redevelopment plan for an area running from the Fox River to Monroe Street, from Cedar Street to a half block south of Main Street.

Then, with ten years of work behind it, the Gregby committee disbanded, and the Redevelopment Authority was created and all the jurisdiction over the project was given to it.

In February 1968, HUD authorized $5.5 million to partially finance the project, and an initial $1.2 million grant was approved.

On March 10, 1969, the first of sixty-six buildings on the property met its fate, as the former A&P Supermarket located on the corner of Jefferson and Cedar was torn down. By May 1972, all land had been purchased and buildings demolished, with the exception of four buildings and six parcels.

After the first contractor fell through, Port Plaza Development Co., out of Whitefish Bay, was selected as the new contractor, and in October 1973, ground was broken on the first retail space. In September 1975, Port Plaza Development Co. walked away from the project, and Chicago-based Port Plaza Mall Co. was appointed. While construction started, financing for the project fell through, and it wasn't until April 1976 that financing was secured and the project got the go-ahead, once again.

Finally, on August 10, 1977, after two decades of work, the Port Plaza Mall opened for business, with two anchor stores—JCPenney and H.C. Prange—and nearly one hundred tenants. A thirty-foot clock on a four-face clock tower from the Winona, Mississippi courthouse was disassembled and transported to the mall site at a cost of $15,000 and became the centerpiece of the new mall.

In 1982, the mall expanded to the south, adding a new food court and a third anchor store: the Boston Store.

In March 1986, Metropolitan Life Insurance purchased the mall. "Metropolitan is starting an aggressive mortgage program, seeking to finance a wide variety of quality projects in excess of $5 million such as shopping centers, high-tech facilities, multi-family housing and leased office buildings," Metropolitan Vice President of Real Estate William J. Bornhoff told the *Press-Gazette* at the time.

In 1988, the mall was home to 119 stores in its one million square feet of space and employed 1,710 people. It underwent a $3 million renovation, adding fountains to the center court area. Four years later, H.C. Prange Co. sold its stores to Younkers, Inc. While the name of the Green Bay store changed, the business remained separate from the mall, as did JCPenney.

In 1997, Zamais Services of Johnstown, Pennsylvania, bought Port Plaza from Metropolitan in a package of ten malls throughout the country. "It's a pretty strong asset," owner Damian Zamias told Thomas Content and Tom Murphy of the *Press-Gazette*. "What we hope to bring to it is some additional stores to improve the small store makeup. We also want to do some things in terms of amenities and aesthetics."

The mall was still 85 percent occupied, but the country was starting to see the indoor mall's decline, as shopping headed toward the suburbs.

In 2001, the City of Green Bay purchased the mall and sold it to Development Associates, which had plans to revitalize it by turning it into a mixed-used space. The mall was renamed Washington Commons, and the fountain and center court area was turned into a food court. Renovations were made through city financing that was to be recouped through special assessment. By that time, just a third of the spaces were leased.

In the fall of 2005, the last two stores—Things Remembered and JCPenney—closed. By March 2006, Development Associates was facing three separate lawsuits.

The property was put up for sale via an agreement between Development Associates, the mortgage holder Baylake Bank, and the City of Green Bay, and the clock tower was returned to Mississippi.

The mall remained vacant, and recycling work began on the building in July 2011. The walls came down in the spring of 2012 to make way for a new Schreiber Foods headquarters.

Chapter 11

DISCOURAGED, BUT NOT DISHEARTENED

Francis "Frank" Henry Hagemeister emigrated from Prussia, first settling in Milwaukee, where he learned the butchering trade while searching for a better life. With a partner, Hagemeister started a small meat business in Green Bay.

"The partners were able to save a little money, with which they intended buying cattle, but Mr. Hagemeister's partner proved dishonest, absconding with the money and leaving the young German with but $23," Ellis Baker Usher wrote in *Wisconsin: Its Story and Biography, 1848–1913*, vol. 8.

Discouraged but not disheartened, Hagemeister started over on his own. Usher continued:

> *It was Mr. Hagemeister's custom, during the early days of his business experience, to make frequent trips through the country, purchasing cattle from farmers, and while on one of the journeys was one day charmed by the beautiful voice of a young lady who was making her way through the woods singing, unconscious of anyone's presence. Mr. Hagemeister was able to make the young lady's acquaintance—she proved to be Miss Barbara Martin, and it was not long afterward that the two were married. That, Mr. Hagemeister always considered was the most fortunate occurrence of his life.*
>
> *Gradually, Mr. Hagemeister worked his way up in the butcher business until 1866, with three other businessmen he erected the buildings and established the Union Brewery on Main Street in the town of Preble.*

He later bought out his partners, Anton Klaus, Herman Mertz, and Joshua Whitney. An October 28, 1871 legal notice shows Hagemeister purchasing one-quarter of the brewery property from Mertz for a sum of $5,500.

In 1872, Hagemeister doubled the size of the brewery's manufacturing area as well as storage space.

"The beer from that institution seems to be popular, and has a large sale in this section of the country," a June 13, 1872 *Press-Gazette* article stated.

One year later, Hagemeister installed a new steam kettle, which tripled its capacity.

Hagemeister and his wife brought six children into the world, and he hoped to give them the opportunities he was not afforded. Frank put his son Henry to work at a young age. Henry then became manager at twenty-four and made a partner at twenty-seven.

In March 1890, letters of incorporation were filed for Hagemeister Brewing Company, with Frank as president and Henry secretary-treasurer. By that time, the company included a facility in Sturgeon Bay as well. That year, the company reported the production of 38,406 barrels of beer—a 42 percent increase from the previous year.

In November 1892, Frank became ill and died; his worth was estimated at $100,000—about $34 million today.

The company continued to expand, including a four-story addition, two large icehouses, two barns, a bottling house, an office, and wagon storage, with three wells on the property by 1907.

Henry served as an alderman and supervisor in the local legislature and in the state assembly (1893–97). He also served as a state senator from 1901 to 1909, and in 1909, he resigned from active management of the company to focus on his work in the financial and real estate industries. Henry died in June 1915.

A couple of years later, U.S. Congress passed the Volstead Act and the country entered the Prohibition era, making it illegal to produce intoxicating liquors.

"Green Bay will, during the next year, become one of the largest ice cream manufacturing cities of the state. The Hagemeister Products company, formerly Hagemeister Brewing Company, will engage in the manufacture of ice cream on a large scale and act as distributor for some of the nationally-known beverages also," a November 1919 *Press-Gazette* article stated.

The articles of incorporation of the old company were amended to change the name to the Hagemeister Products Company and to enlarge its line of business. The article continued, "Under the amended constitution, the state gives the company authority to manufacture, market and prepare for market, sell and deal in foods and edibles, the brewing of malt and cereal beverages, the manufacture of health products."

In June 1925, the Green Bay Hagemeister plant was raided by federal Prohibition marshals. The raid came after a shipment of beer was discovered being transported from Green Bay to Hurley. After locating what the federal officers determined was "good beer," seven men were arrested, and injunction proceedings to padlock the facility began.

Company management issued the following statement in response: "None of the officers or directors of the Hagemeister Food Products company were aware of the fact that this beer was being sold. About a month ago, we put a young man in charge of our soda water department, and in his zeal to make a good showing in receipts, he apparently began selling beer. We were told today that the beer was being sold to runners from the northern part of the state when the arrests were made last night."

Later that month, receivers were appointed for the company to protect the interest of its creditors and bondholders, and months later, involuntary bankruptcy proceedings were started by three of its creditors. The company started reorganization plans, adding butter and cheese to its products; but on February 10, 1926, the plant was put up for sale. All bids were deemed inadequate.

In April 1926, articles of incorporation papers were filed for the new successor to the Hagemeister products: Bellevue Food Products.

Later that year, liens on the Hagemeister property were filed in federal court against the company for failure to pay taxes. This would cause ongoing issues for locally organized Valley Brewing and Refrigerating Company, which was looking to secure the property. In 1934, the Hagemeister facility was closed.

Today, Schreiber Foods exists on the grounds that once served as home to the Green Bay brewery.

Chapter 12

A MONUMENT TO THE FIDELITY OF THE ODD FELLOWS

Bearing its massive tower toward the heavens, a monument to the fidelity of the Independent Order of Odd Fellows of Wisconsin to their pledge to provide for the widows and orphans of deceased brothers, the $30,000 Widows and Orphans Home stands on Astor Heights overlooking this city, complete and ready to receive those for whom it was created," the *Green Bay Weekly Gazette* stated in January 1891.

"The heart of every Odd Fellow of Wisconsin swells with pride at the work that has been successfully accomplished and the voices of those widows and mothers who will be shielded and provided with a comfortable home in which to spend their declining years and rear their children."

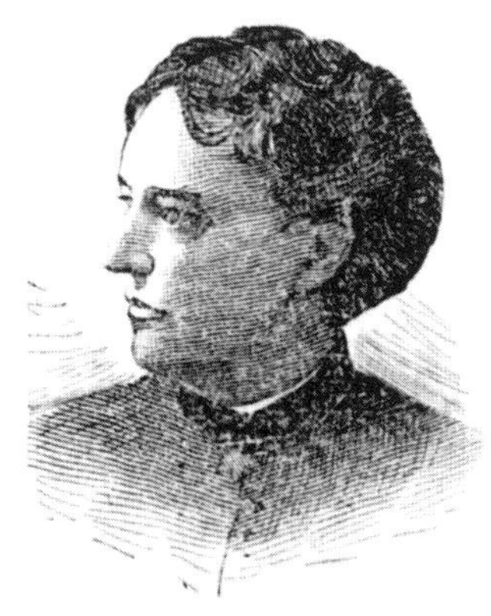

Sarah E. Hutchinson was the first matron of the home. *Public domain.*

The Green Bay Odd Fellow Home was just the sixteenth institution to be developed by the group since the first Odd Fellows order was formed in the United States in Baltimore in 1819 with a mission "to render assistance to every brother, in sickness of distress." The first Wisconsin Odd Fellow Lodge was established in 1835 when the state was still part of the Iowa Territory.

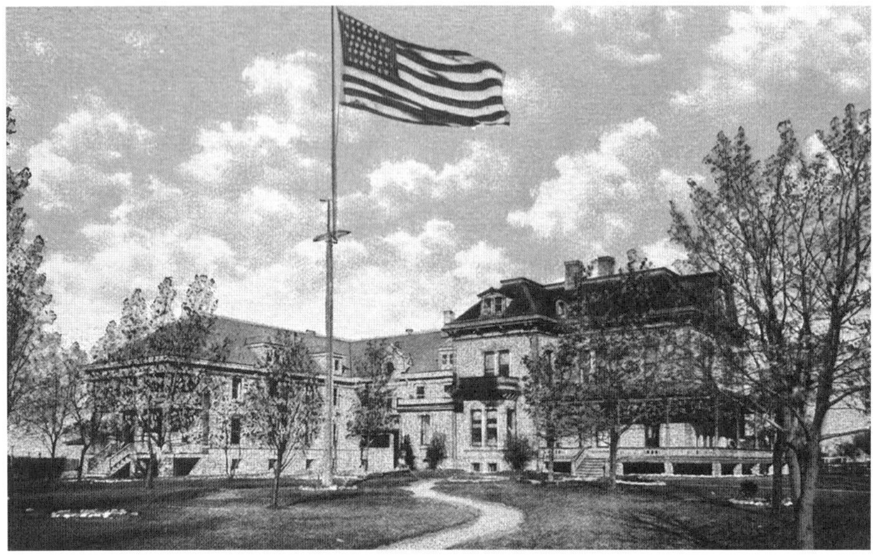

The Green Bay Odd Fellows Home was just the sixteenth institution to be developed by the group since the first Odd Fellows order was formed in the United States. *Historical postcard.*

In 1889, a Wisconsin Grand Lodge of Odd Fellows committee began investigating the establishment of a home for the aging, widowed, and orphaned children of its members in Green Bay. One year later, land near the Fox River was purchased with an existing facility present. A statuesque building was constructed there and dedicated on January 23, 1891, on what became 822 Grignon Street, Green Bay.

During the dedication, Mayor James H. Elmore, Green Bay's twenty-sixth mayor, spoke of its mission:

> *We all know that among primitive nations, woman is but a slave and that the progress of her status in the world has been slow, that it is not only now, that it can be fairly said that among civilized nations woman is the admitted equal companion of man.*
>
> *Therefore, the establishment of an Odd Fellows Woman's Home, although its benefits are to be made to extend to children and indigent males, means something more than the establishment of an ordinary charitable or benevolent institution. It is a departure from the usual methods of dispensing charity, even in this great country of charities.*

Throughout the following decades, the facility provided a home and education for orphans and nursing services to its aging members. Many of those who passed at the facility were buried on a plot owned by the Odd Fellow Lodge at Woodlawn Cemetery in Green Bay.

In 1966, the facility was licensed as a skilled care facility and opened to the public.

In the summer of 1975, the Brown County Health Planning Council approved the allocation of $950,000 to replace the aging facility with a new structure on the same property, while the previous structure was scheduled for removal. The new facility remains at the adjacent location at 1229 South Jackson Street, Green Bay.

Chapter 13

BROWN COUNTY COMES TOGETHER TO COMBAT TUBERCULOSIS

In 1882, Dr. Robert Koch announced the discovery of the germ that caused tuberculosis (TB)—Mycobacterium tuberculosis—but in the early 1900s, tuberculosis of the lungs was still one of the leading causes of death in the United States.

In 1912, the National Association for the Study and Prevention of Tuberculosis said that almost $19 million—about $619 million today—was spent on an "anti-tuberculosis campaign." However, the number of cases in Green Bay continued to increase, and the community began urging county government to research the possibility of a county sanatorium in order to isolate the transmittable disease.

County legislation in those days was slower, as the county board met on a semiannual basis. A resolution to create the sanatorium was presented in 1912 but shot down. On November 19, 1913, a resolution was introduced again by Fred Altmayer, of De Pere, but was deferred until the next day of their typical three-day county board session. The resolution appropriated funding for the purchase of land and construction of a hospital and was passed 18–16 that Friday.

"After much parleying regarding the amount to be appropriated whether it should be $25,000 or $20,000—a vote was taken and passed," a *Press-Gazette* article stated.

A three-member Sanatorium Committee was appointed to find an appropriate plot of land, with Altmayer as chair. The committee selected several sites on both sides of the Fox River at the junction of Green Bay and De Pere, as well as other spots in both communities. In February

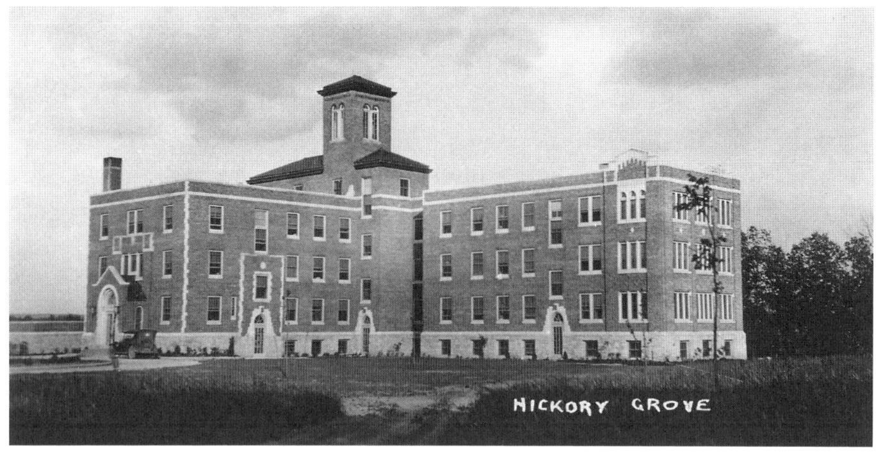

There was much debate over where to build the new tuberculosis facility, but the state board and the community eventually decided on the same property as the first building. *De Pere Historical Society photo.*

1914, the state board of control came to view the selected properties, and a site along the west side of the Fox River in the town of Lawrence was ultimately selected. One likely advantage was its proximity to the Chicago & Northwestern rail line, which ran adjacent to the property's west side.

"The sanatorium will provide rooms for 20 regular patients with a capacity for 12 more by using two large rooms as wards. The construction will be of concrete and plaster frames. The building will be in a 'T' shape....The building will consist of two stories and a basement," an April 1914 edition of the *Green Bay Semi-Weekly Gazette* stated.

"There will be a large sleeping porch surrounding the sanatorium, an office, sitting rooms, examination room, private dining room for the employees. There is a flowing well on the site acquired for the sanatorium and an ample supply of cold water will be assured."

In February 1915, the facility began taking its first patients.

THE EXPANSION

The following year, the community came together once again and through paid subscription purchased a twenty-five-foot boat, the *Minnie S.*, for the facility; it was big enough for fifteen passengers. Weeks later, a motor was purchased for the boat. The boat was renamed *Old Hickory* and floated in the Fox River as "a monument to the splendid spontaneity and spirit of broadmindedness of the true American, an unselfish acknowledgment of the material needs of unfortunate fellow Americans," patients and staff stated in a thank-you letter published in the *Press-Gazette* that year.

In October 1921, with tuberculosis still claiming lives, Brown County physicians, the women's clubs of De Pere and Green Bay, county board representatives, Hickory Grove trustees, and other interested regional community members met to discuss enlarging the facility and including Door and Kewaunee Counties. This idea was supported by the Wisconsin Anti-Tuberculosis Association.

It wasn't until 1926, however, that the county board began work on expansion to accommodate a growing waiting list. There was much debate over where to build the new facility, but the state board and the community eventually decided on the same property as the first building.

In March 1927, the Brown County Board voted to borrow $250,000 to build the additional structure, which would be a three-story building with three sets of bathrooms on each floor and sun porches on the front and ends. On the third floor, an open plaza area would lead to the bell tower, with a bell that would toll every hour. Once constructed, a forty-five-foot tunnel would connect the old building with the new.

The original building was to remain on the property to house the staff, but as transportation became a household option, workers began to commute. In September 1929, the forty-three patients at the facility were moved to the new building. By March 1936, one hundred tuberculosis patients were being attended to at the facility.

Earlier that year, the county had taken advantage of the Works Progress Administration—which created jobs during the Great Depression—to remodel and repair the old building to segregate the more severe cases from the less affected patients.

In December 1956, with a max capacity of eighty-six, the patient number sat at eighty, while the facility played host to patients from other counties in northeast Wisconsin.

In 1955, Hickory Grove was one of just eighteen county sanatoria in the state. By 1957, that number was down to seventeen.

In 1971, the second floor of the sanatorium was converted into a nursing home facility. "The patient population at the facility has declined regularly in recent years because of diagnosing, treating and preventing tuberculosis and currently the staff at the sanatorium outnumbers its patients by two to one," a December 15, 1971 *Press-Gazette* article stated.

AN UNCERTAIN FUTURE

In September 1971, the sanatorium housed forty-five patients—just twenty-three with tuberculosis—and the county began to make budget cuts to the facility.

The following year began with ninety-one employees on the payroll, a number the county hoped to get down to sixty-two or sixty-five by the end of the year. By the end of the year, Hickory Grove was being promoted as an extended-care facility, with the chronically ill assigned to one floor.

As the original building was declining, there was talk of razing the 1915 structure. In 1973, the county board approved the demolition of the building and work to cap off the basement of the structure, as it could still be reached from the tunnel and used for storage.

But the institution's future still hung in the balance. While the second building's future remained a source of discussion for the county board, there was no doubt at the time that the institution would have its place in history. "You'd be surprised how many families have had someone out at the sanatorium at one time or another," said Wisconsin Sanatorium Trustees Association President and Green Bay resident Loris Dow.

In June 1974, Brown County Mental Health Center inpatient administrator Lynn Lucia was appointed to head the new Hickory Grove Study Committee to find "recommendations and alternatives" for the facility. At that time, there were approximately thirty-four nursing home patients and fifteen TB patients. The study came back the following month with a recommendation to phase out the sanatorium. By November 1974, the name was changed to Hickory Grove Nursing Home as the county looked for proposals from licensed nursing home administrators to run the home.

However, the facility needed a greater purpose to reduce a $240,000 operational deficit with just thirty-four patients. To convert it into an operation that could function at its highest level as a nursing home—a sixty-eight-bed skilled nursing facility—would cost $600,000.

The county ultimately decided to close the facility on August 31, 1974. The following year, the remaining building and sixteen acres were sold to Elroy Nero and Raphael Parins, of Green Bay, for use as a supper club/hotel business later noted as the Playboy Club. But issues with the DNR and the sewage system put that development to a stop.

In 1984, Al Pokel Jr. purchased the property with plans to develop a veal-processing operation. When that met with opposition, Pokel refocused on luxury apartments. But Hickory Grove continued to sit empty into the early

1990s, when the Brown County Sheriff's Department and other community members called for its demolition.

"There's no way they're going to remodel it," Brown County Sheriff's Captain Frank Tomcheck told the *Press-Gazette*'s Julie Bell. "It's just too far gone. Floors are missing in places and elevator shafts are open," he added. The windows were also all smashed out, and graffiti lined the walls.

The building was torn down in the late 1990s. The property is now home to Hickory Grove Heights.

Chapter 14

GREEN BAY'S FIRST SKYSCRAPER

On May 27, 1903, the creation of a new three-story building on the northeast corner of Washington and Cherry Streets in Green Bay hit the pages of the *Press-Gazette*. Initial plans called for a building "two stores in width" that would take the footprint of Henry D. Wilner's existing building and the Cent store and Wisconsin Telephone Company next door.

A week later, the plans went through and the first tenant was announced: Henry Herrick and Henry Van, who would operate a "first-class clothing house" on the first floor. The plans for Wilner's new building would be handled by architect J.E. Clancy, with construction of the now four-story building handled by Thomas Roy.

"The new building will be of solid brick with a pressed brick or other ornamental front," a *Press-Gazette* article read. "The front will be of plate [wood] extending across the two stores with a large entrance in the center of the building."

The Knox & Wilner shoe store, which had been operating on the site, was temporarily moved to the Funke building on the corner of Main and Adams Streets.

As demand grew for office space in the city, Wilner soon looked to add fifth and sixth stories.

"At the present time, but the southern half of the building—22 feet in width—can be built. The Cent store and the Wisconsin Telephone Company have leases of the other side of the building which prevent any work on it for the present," a July 31, 1903 *Press-Gazette* article stated. "In order to raise the northern half of the building, the north wall of the present building will have to be rebuilt and this will of course necessitate the vacating of the building."

After much debate, an October 1903 *Press-Gazette* article announced that Green Bay would have its first "sky scraper." "The south 22 feet of the Wilner corner will be run up the six stories in height as planned," it stated.

By the end of the year, the odd-looking building was ready for occupation.

On January 9, 1908, as the clock started a new day, firemen were battling a blaze that had broken out in the six-story building. A southeast wind fanned the flames as the firemen fought to keep the blaze that started in the basement confined to the main floor. However, by the time they had control over the fire, it had reached five adjoining buildings downtown, causing $45,000 in damage ($1.5 million today). Wilner lived in a room in the building and was able to get out through a fire escape.

In October 1921, in what was defined as one of the largest real estate transactions to occur in the city's downtown to date, Henry Herrick purchased the building from Wilner at a cost of $80,000.

In the summer of 1926, suffering from an attack of the "flu" and, according to newspaper reports, "refusing to go to the hospital," the man who built Green Bay's first skyscraper passed away at the age of sixty-five.

Three years later, the Herrick Clothing Company made plans to move the store to an expanded space in the City Center building at Adams and Main Streets—the last store to vacate the six-story building.

"The company was the first, and will be the last tenant in the 'Wilner Skyscraper' since the building is to be razed immediately upon their departure," a November 19, 1929 *Press-Gazette* article stated.

"The site has been leased by the F.W. Woolworth company for a period of 50 years, and it is the announced plans of the new company to raze the present building and erect a new one suited to the needs of the company."

In early February 1930, the crews began to demolish the building. Crushed brick from the razed structure was used to fill the road to the cottages east of Green Bay's Bay View Beach.

Chapter 15

THE LODGE OF FATHERS

The Benevolent and Protective Order of Elks (BPOE) was founded in New York City on February 16, 1868, by a small group of actors and entertainers as a social organization. As the concept spread throughout the country, its membership broadened to include businessmen, professionals, and those of other occupations.

On March 15, 1893, a BPOE lodge was founded with twenty-eight men in the city of Green Bay in Odd Fellows Hall.

"Some read the initials to mean 'the best people on earth.' This is all right, but BPOE in reality means the Benevolent and Protective Order of Elks," a *State Gazette* article stated the following day.

"There has been a movement for some time past to organize a lodge of this order in Green Bay, but for certain reasons, the matter was not made public."

On December 6, the order held its first social, sending out four hundred invitations for the complimentary event at Turner Hall. Exalted Ruler S.J. Murphy Jr. told the crowd:

> *This event will be recorded in the papers tomorrow as the first public Social Session given by the Green Bay Lodge, No. 259, of the Benevolent and Protective Order of Elks. It is customary on an occasion like this for the Exalted Ruler or some other gifted brother to give a short address, and as the gifted brother is not present I shall have to make the speech myself.*

Although this is a secret organization, we are very glad that the public can at times share with us one of its most prominent features.

This order is founded on the grand principles of justice, charity, brotherly love and fidelity. We have tried to do justice to the good taste of the musical people of Green Bay, and we have no doubt that you will do justice to the entertainment and give it such praise as its merits demand.

The Elks held their first meetings at the Knights of Pythias Hall in the Duchateau building on Main Street in Green Bay until 1902, when they moved to their own building on the corner of Jefferson and Cherry Streets. The two-story building cost $15,000—raised by subscriptions—and its first floor contained a lounging and reception room in the front of the building with two large fireplaces. The back of the first floor was home to the club room, a billiard and card room, a kitchen, a cloakroom, and a secretary's office. The second floor contained a large lodge room—which was also used as a dance hall—and a stage. The basement was home to four bowling lanes and showers.

Work on the clubhouse began in July 1901, and it was officially dedicated in February 1902. According to the Elks, it was the first Elks clubhouse built in the state of Wisconsin, and the building brought a sense of pride, along with the changing attitude in how they operated.

"Twenty years ago, the Elks were characteristically of social activities bent more or less on frivolity. In the 20 years passed, it has grown to mature manhood—gray hairs have tinged its temples. Today, its name is the synonym of dignified, unostentatious charity, where it was the lodge of sons, it is now the lodge of fathers," members of the leadership said in a February 1916 editorial.

The clubhouse played host to many club meetings, social events, memorial services, and productions for five decades before the Elks looked to expand.

"Meetings, conventions and social affairs of all kinds were held in the redbrick building with the white-pillared, two-story veranda," Green Bay historian Jack Rudolph wrote in 1968. "The total number of dances and parties held there—only a fraction by the Elks themselves—boggles the imagination."

"Half a century of constant use took its toll on the building. As early as 1939 it was obvious that a replacement would be needed but it wasn't until 1957 that the project really got into gear."

Work on a new lodge on the corner of South Adams and Crooks Streets was started on October 25, 1958, and the property on which the original

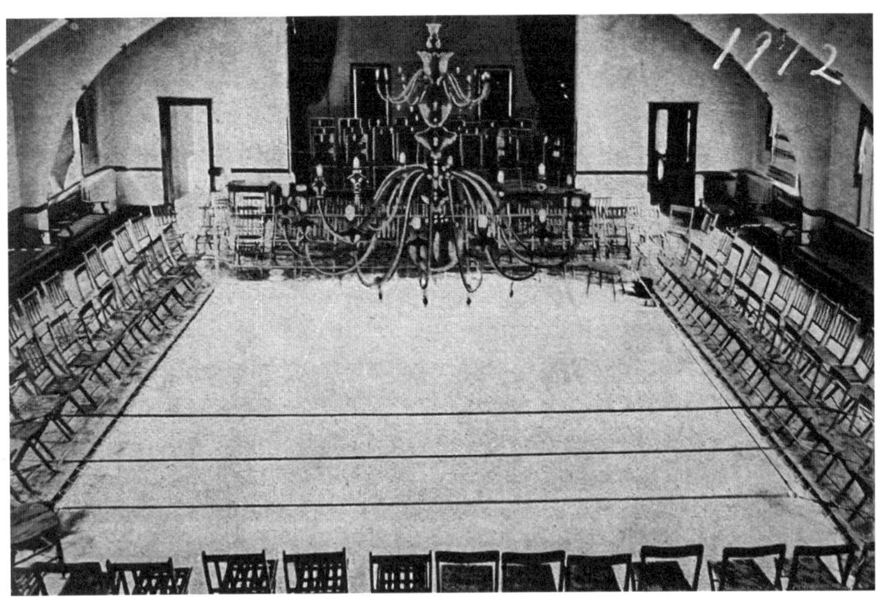

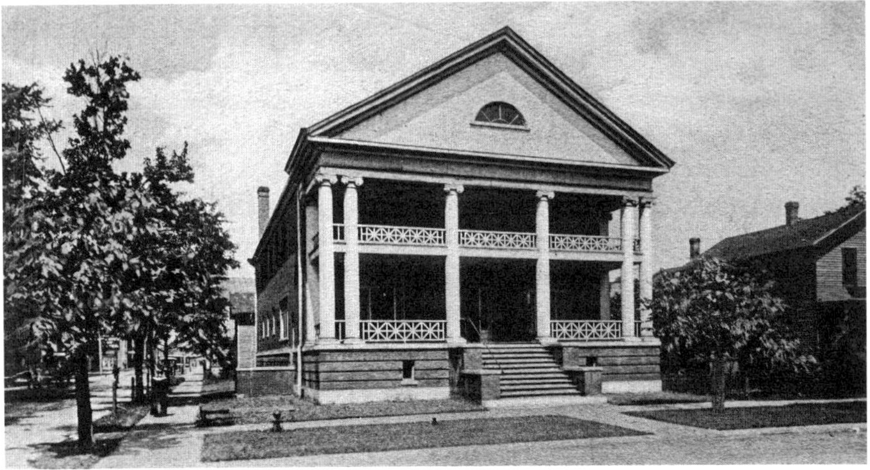

Top: The clubhouse played host to many club meetings, social events, memorial services, and productions for five decades. *Dick and Darlene Charneski collection.*

Bottom: Work on the clubhouse began in July 1901, and it was officially dedicated in February 1902. According to the Elks, it was the first Elks clubhouse built in the state of Wisconsin. *Historical postcard.*

clubhouse sat was sold. The project took one year to construct and several years to fundraise for the facility, which cost somewhere in the neighborhood of a half million dollars.

In the new facility, the Elks would hit the height of their membership—reported at 1,400. But later, as numbers dwindled, the lodge moved to its current location on South Ridge Road in Ashwaubenon.

Chapter 16

THE CITY BEAUTIFUL MOVEMENT REACHES GREEN BAY

Bay Beach Amusement Park has been welcoming families for well over a century, but the inspiration behind the park dates back further to June 1895, when the Green Bay Business Men's Association was pushed toward the development of the property at Bay Beach.

"It is the intention of the association to push the work of developing a summer resort at the beach. An arrangement has been made with the Kewaunee, Green Bay & Western Road for the securing of eighty carloads of gravel. This will be dumped alongside the track at 12th Street and hauled from there by team [horses] and used to cover the surface of the boulevard leading to the shore," a June 1895 *Green Bay Press-Gazette* article stated.

"Already many people from this city drive out to the beach for the purpose of enjoying the splendid bathing. With the building of a first-class hotel there and the improvement of the surroundings, it will undoubtedly become a favorite resort for summer tourists."

Plans weren't developed, however, until the summer of 1899, when the Preble Town Board approved a street railway franchise through the town in the name of Patrick Glynn. Glynn was also backing Captain J.A. Cusick, who was planning and engineering the project.

Early sketches of the grounds showed "a casino for summer theatrical purposes, a pavilion for band concerts and dances, bathing houses and a modernly equipped bathhouse, a pier and baseball, golf and lawn tennis grounds….A handsome park is to be laid out between the casino and pavilion. The proposed hotel will not be built this year," a June 1899 *Green Bay Semi-Weekly Gazette* article said.

At that time, many amusement parks were being constructed around the country. The World's Columbian Exposition of 1893 and its "White City" had left its impression, and those who visited Chicago during the fair took home new ideas. This helped usher in the City Beautiful movement.

In April 1900, work began on the hotel at what would become Bay View Beach in Green Bay.

"Work on the summer hotel to be built by M.R. Nejedlo, at Bay Beach, was begun this morning," the April 3, 1900 *Press-Gazette* stated. "The hotel is to be built on the west side of the boulevard, in the grove of willows between the small bridge and the shore."

The hotel was described as a large, roomy building with a broad porch with a balcony above it, extending around three sides of the structure.

Work on the bathhouses began in May and was completed in June, along with a small pier. At the same time, subscriptions were being asked to improve the roads leading to the resort.

By July, Nejedlo was advertising his new resort at the "foot of North 12th Street."

That fall, Cusick entered into a contract with Nejedlo to run boats to and from the resort.

In July 1901, Nejedlo began work on an existing dance hall, tearing out the rear portion to create a stage in order to host vaudeville performances. During the same month, Cusick and Dominick Hagerty opened the first amusement rides at the resort: chutes, or toboggan boats that would slide down a long ramp into the water. That summer, the pavilion was also completed.

In 1911, the Bay View Beach Amusement Park filed its articles of incorporation, listing Frank Murphy, Joseph Servotte, and William Hoberg as the incorporators, purchased by Murphy and Rahr. Cusick had left in 1916 to work for Green Bay's Indian Packing Company.

In 1920, Murphy and Rahr donated the park to the city—buildings included—with a stipulation that it remain a park. The city changed the name from Bay View Beach to Bay Beach.

In 1924, city park department staff moved the bathhouse two hundred feet to the east and turned it so it was parallel with the shore.

The following year, they worked to remodel the facility, splitting it in two sections—one for men and one for women—with an entrance in the middle. During construction, the building was cut in two, and a new section was built to connect the two sides.

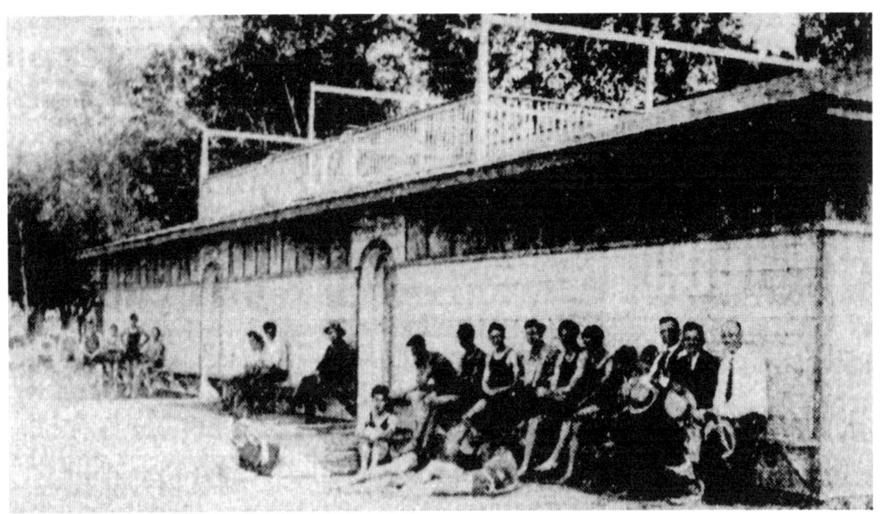

The lumber from the damaged bathhouse was gathered and stored, and plans were drawn up to build a smaller structure with the salvaged wood, at a cost of $1,200. Press-Gazette *photo*.

"The new section will be covered with a roof with gables at right angles to the ridge line on the main building and extending a few feet beyond the present wall line. The new roof will be supported by a row of six pillars instead of by a wall thus relieving the long lines of the length of the building," a *Press-Gazette* article stated.

In October 1929, a storm swept through the area, causing flooding and about $150,000 of damage to bay-area homes. The bathhouse was completely damaged and found resting against a nearby building.

The lumber from the bathhouse was gathered and stored, and plans were drawn up to build a smaller structure with the salvaged wood, at a cost of $1,200. The unexpected expense canceled plans for the construction of two tennis courts that year.

The new bathhouse was opened in time for the summer 1930 season.

Chapter 17

THE MINAHAN BUILDING

A Downtown Hub for Professionals

In February 1906, negotiations were in progress for the purchase of the American House property on the corner of Walnut and Washington Streets in downtown Green Bay just east of the Fox River.

The purchasers—sitting mayor R.E. Minahan, V.I. Minahan, and E.R. Minahan—had big plans for the property: a six-story store and office building. The group incorporated as the "Minahan Building Company" and purchased the property. However, due to the high cost of materials, the Minahans pulled back on the project and sold the property to Ed Garot.

"The barn in the rear will be moved to a vacant lot on South Washington Street as will the building material in the hotel when it is torn down," a September 5, 1906 *Green Bay Semi-Weekly Gazette* article stated.

"Mr. Garot has not definitely decided what he will do with the property but it is known that a large building will be erected there next spring. It is thought that he will move his plumbing shop to the building when it is completed and branch out into a larger jobbing business."

By January 1907, plans for the Minahans' new building were back on for that property. The company was incorporated for $150,000—over $5 million today—by John R. Minahan, V.I. Minahan, and R.E. Minahan.

"The structure will be a six-story fireproof, reinforced concrete office building. It will be of brick—cream colored," a *Press-Gazette* article stated.

The building would be large enough to offer seventy-five to eighty offices, with two main entrances—one on Washington and one on Walnut.

Garot decided to expand his business at 224 Cherry Street. Once constructed, the Minahan Building became a hub for downtown business, housing the offices of banks, insurance companies, accountants, brokerage companies, doctors, dentists, lawyers, and more.

When the Minahans objected to the high rates of the power company, they next worked to construct their own plant to provide electricity to the downtown district in the basement of the structure.

In May 1907, an application for a "franchise to construct, operate and maintain suitable conduits in the streets and alleys in the downtown portion of Green Bay for the purpose of furnishing electric current for light and power uses, hot water, steam and air was made by the Minahan Building Company," a *Press-Gazette* article stated.

It was approved that July by the Green Bay City Council "without a word of discussion during the meeting and without a dissenting vote" for a period of twenty years at its 205 East Walnut Street location. Work began on the utilities in the fall of 1908.

But the Wisconsin Public Service soon went after the Minahan company in a legal battle, as they tried to bar them from operation. The battle went to the state supreme court, where in November 1909 a decision was reached to annul the power and light franchise granted to the Minahan Building Company.

On September 12, 1913, a Wisconsin Public Service notice was released to area media stating:

> *The Wisconsin Public Service Company has acquired the electric and power property of the Minahan Building Company and has this day taken possession of and is operating the same.*
>
> *The steam power plant of the Minahan Building Company will be discontinued at the earliest possible moment so as to put a stop to wasteful operations, whose financial loss would have brought early bankruptcy to an organization of less ample financial strength than the Minahan Building Company.*

Green Bay Gas & Electric promised to provide service to the Minahan customers, making the conversion at its own expense.

From 1910 to 1945, the U.S. Weather Service operated from the fifth floor of the statuesque building. "The department had its wind instruments, temperature and rainfall gauges on the roof and issued its daily weather reports from the building," a March 4, 1984 *Press-Gazette* article recalled.

In 1931, the building underwent an extensive ten-month remodeling and hosted a formal reopening in October. A *Press-Gazette* article stated:

> *The modern and modernistic are glorified in the entire scheme and effect of the new Minahan Building interior. The ground floor lobby and all of the corridors on the six floors above it are done in a color scheme of silver and black. The black is a shining black Vitrolite, a new product featured in very many of the newest Chicago business towers, but no large installation of which had been made in Green Bay before.*
>
> *On the black Vitrolite walls of the lobby, two scenes have been etched, one depicting "Historic Green Bay" and the other "Industrial Green Bay." For the former, the artist chose the landing of Nicolet, the first White man in the "New West," and the latter shows Main St. Bridge with its two bascule lifts admitting a huge lake freighter and in the background, the towering stacks of mills and factories.*

In 1941, the building's owner, John R. Minahan, died and left the building to his nephew, Victor McCormick. The building was later renamed the Minahan-McCormick Building.

"Generally reclusive, McCormick broke ties with many old friends after his marriage in 1970 to Dorice Dupuis. In 1978, she was given power of attorney over the estate of her husband, whose health had declined. In 1980, a judge said the estate had been mismanaged. By the time of his death, McCormick's one-time fortune of $22 million had shrunk to approximately $600,000," a 1987 *Press-Gazette* article stated.

In the summer of 1983, Green Bay officials began considering purchasing and razing the building, which had been listed for sale for three years, had just thirteen tenants, and was now under the control of the Kellogg-Citizens National Bank. With the planned reconstruction of the Walnut Street Bridge, which was scheduled to begin in January 1985, the city needed a wider intersection for turn lanes at Walnut and Washington, just east of the bridge.

"The city worked for two years with the owner of the Bellin Building and the trustees of the Minahan-McCormick Building on a proposal to build a walkway through the Walnut Street sides of each building. That plan would have eliminated the need for demolition. But the Bellin Building's owner was concerned the project could cause structural damage to his building," a *Press-Gazette* article stated.

An offer was made in October, and the property was sold to the Green Bay Redevelopment Authority for $230,000 late that month. The building was demolished in March 1984.

Chapter 18

A HOUSE AHEAD OF ITS TIME

In 1835, the town of Astor was platted, the proprietors being John Jacob Astor, Ramsay Crooks and Robert Stuart. A fine hotel, the Astor House, was built by John Jacob Astor, on the corner of Adams and Mason streets, and also a rambling structure, known in later years as 'the bank building.' Where the first regularly incorporated financial institution west of Detroit, the Bank of Wisconsin, opened its doors in 1835," Ella Hoes Neville et al. wrote in *Historic Green Bay*.

"At the time the shrewd old fur dealer, John Jacob Astor, desiring to increase the value of the land he owned in the new village of Astor, and to draw here some of the settlers who were coming in numbers to this part of the country, wisely determined to build a fine hotel, in which the transient guest should be made so comfortable he might be changed into a permanent resident," Fannie C. Last said before the Green Bay Historical Society on December 2, 1901.

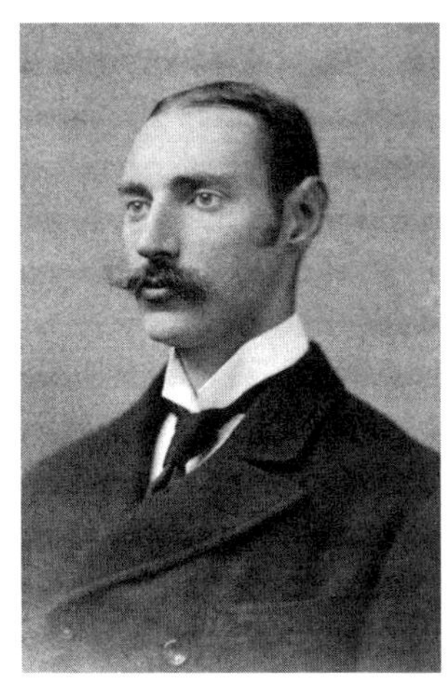

John Jacob Astor. *Public domain.*

"Chicago at that time had but some fifty inhabitants all told; and the little village of Astor, which was to be honored with this edifice, so far superior in size and in other respects to anything to be found in all the broad expanse of the Northwest, contained not more than some half dozen houses, built mostly of logs, small in size and destitute of paint."

Astor hired James Duane Doty as his agent and promoter. Since the adjacent village of Navarino had a hotel, "Doty wanted one so far superior to the primitive Washington House that it would be a frontier sensation," Green Bay historian Jack Rudolph wrote in 1958. Construction on the hotel began in the spring of 1837.

Last said:

> *About the time the Astor House was erected the Astor warehouse and dock were built near it—a convenient landing place for boats coming up the lakes or down the river. Much interest must have centered just here during the busy months of preparation and construction, and small as was the population in the two villages one can imagine quite a wild excitement when the work was actually completed, and in all the imposing majesty of its three stories and crowning cupola, the Astor House glistening fresh white paint, stood in the morning sunshine, a beautiful object to the partial eyes of the beholders. Perhaps a stranger would hardly have considered it an architectural gem; it was very large, very square, quite guiltless of any adornment or frivolous devices whatever. Its many windows were provided with bright green blinds to temper sun and wind to the lambs gathered within its walls.*
>
> *The spacious, comfortable rooms became a favorite meeting place for the citizens. Here the gentlemen of the twin villages were wont to assemble in the evening for the interchange of ideas, the discussion of the news of the day, and here the village storyteller enlivened the evening with copious recollections of his past life, and predictions, cheerful or otherwise, according to his mood, of the future.*

The hotel opened in August 1837, coinciding with the country's Panic of 1837—a major recession in the U.S. economy—which rippled through the nation until the mid-1840s.

"Gradually, time caught up with the hotel and it began to justify Doty's vision. The rising lumber industry and the tide of immigration during the late 1840s and 1850s turned it into a highly profitable venture," Rudolph stated.

In 1854, the hotel was purchased by Ira Stone. "He completely redecorated it, added rooms, enlarged the stables and imported a 'Troy coach' that became Green Bay's first public transportation and which he used to transport guests to and from the ship landings," added Rudolph.

Again, the hotel was operating way ahead of its time, but good fortune would not last.

Last said:

> *The old house lost none of its popularity while Mr. Stone presided over it, and it was very prosperous and successful financially. Shortly before its destruction, it was decided to enlarge the hotel, giving fourteen new rooms in addition to the number it already contained. It became quite a popular abiding place for families who preferred boarding to the cares and worries of housekeeping. Lieutenant Smith, later Admiral Smith, who after doing gallant service during the Civil War, spent his last years in Green Bay, boarded here for some time with his wife, the gayest and most social of women, who made life in the little city one perpetual festival while she sojourned in our midst. Col. Robinson brought his bride here, a very welcome addition not only to the Astor House, but to Green Bay society as well. Perhaps the old house was too prosperous for its own good; certainly, it made for itself an enemy. Several unsuccessful attempts to burn it were followed by one better or worse planned, for this time the flames had made great headway before being discovered, and the house was burnt to the ground one night in August 1857.*
>
> *So rapidly did the old house burn that the inmates barely escaped with their lives, leaving their possessions behind them. Mrs. Smith, genius of gayety and fun, came down the stairs while they were in flames, and a few moments after her descent they fell in ruins.*

The Green Bay Common Council offered a $3,000 reward for information on the arsonist who set fire to the structure. "The reward is a liberal one, as it should be, and we hope, for the good of the community, that it will prove to be sufficient for the purpose. Even should it fail, as we have no doubt it will, it will be some satisfaction to know that the city authorities have done all they could in the matter," the August 27, 1857 *Green Bay Advocate* stated.

Historical publications do not provide any indication that the perpetrator was identified, but fingers were being pointed. The *Green Bay Weekly Gazette* stated in September 1893:

> *After the fire, a good share of the members of the fire department, taking some of the fire apparatus along, went across East River and tore down a house of unsavory repute.*
>
> *This was done partly on general principles and partly from a lurking suspicion that there was some connection between the Astor House fire and the inmates or frequenters of the house they destroyed.*

Chapter 19

THE BEAUMONT

Yesterday's Premier Hotel

The Beaumont Hotel stood on the corner of Main and North Washington Streets for a century, but its history goes back to the settlement of a village that has long been swallowed up by the city of Green Bay.

"When Daniel Whitney platted his village of Navarino in 1830 one of his first projects was a hotel which he named the Washington House. He built it on the northeast corner of Washington and Main," Green Bay historian Jack Rudolph wrote in 1963.

> *Whitney's Washington House, one of the first hotels in Wisconsin, lasted nearly 25 years. It escaped destruction in the disastrous fire of 1853, which wiped out much of the Washington Street business district, only to go up in flames a year later.*
>
> *Most of the time it was owned by the famous Army surgeon Dr. William Beaumont, who bought the property from Whitney in about 1834.*

Beaumont leased the hotel to a string of managers. When William died in 1853, it was passed down to his son Israel Green "Bud" Beaumont.

After the 1854 building fire, the property sat vacant until 1860. That year, Israel and his partner/brother-in-law, Alfred Pelton, began construction of a four-story hotel on the property. The hotel was nearly completed when the Civil War broke out in April 1861.

The hotel opened during the summer of 1864 before construction was completed. It was not fully completed until 1865. It was named the Beaumont House in memory of Israel's father.

Rudolph wrote:

> *Beaumont was a likable and popular man but a bust as a publican. The hotel sank deeper into the red until he was finally forced to borrow $7,500 from his friend Henry Furber, president of the Charter Oak Life Insurance Co. That was a staggering debt in 1876.*
>
> *Furber took a mortgage on the property, made out to the insurance company, as security. A few years later, when Beaumont was unable to pay, he foreclosed, and Bud lost the hotel.*

In October 1896, Henry Bertram picked up the hotel with plans to build it back even stronger.

In the summer of 1909, work began on a fifth story and an addition on the north side of the building at a cost of about $275,000—nearly $10 million today. At completion, the hotel would have two hundred guest rooms—eighty of them with connected baths and eighty with a shower bath.

"Every room will have running hot and cold water and will be equipped with a telephone," a 1909 *Press-Gazette* article stated.

"The first story of both the old and new parts of the hotel will be pressed brick. One more story will be added to the present part, making it five stories high, and the addition in the rear will be five stories in height."

Shortly after that, the Bertrams were ready to retire and sold the newly renovated property to Frederic G. Hall. "A former superintendent of the Harvel railroad chain, Hall gave the Beaumont dining room a national reputation," Rudolph explained. "In 1912, Hall brought A.C. Witteborg from Chicago to manage the hotel. When Hall died a few years later, Witteborg formed a group of employees to buy the Beaumont from the estate."

In January 1963, Beaumont manager Carl Witteborg, A.C.'s son, announced that the century-old landmark would be torn down to make way for a one-hundred-room motor inn to be affiliated with Parkway Inns. The hotel held its last night on February 28, 1963. Demolition of the historic building began the following month.

Officers of the new Beaumont Motor Inn were President/Manager Carl Witteborg; Joseph Whalen and Charles H. Mitchell of Parkway Inns; and Ray Smith Jr. The Beaumont Motor Inn opened on August 8, 1965.

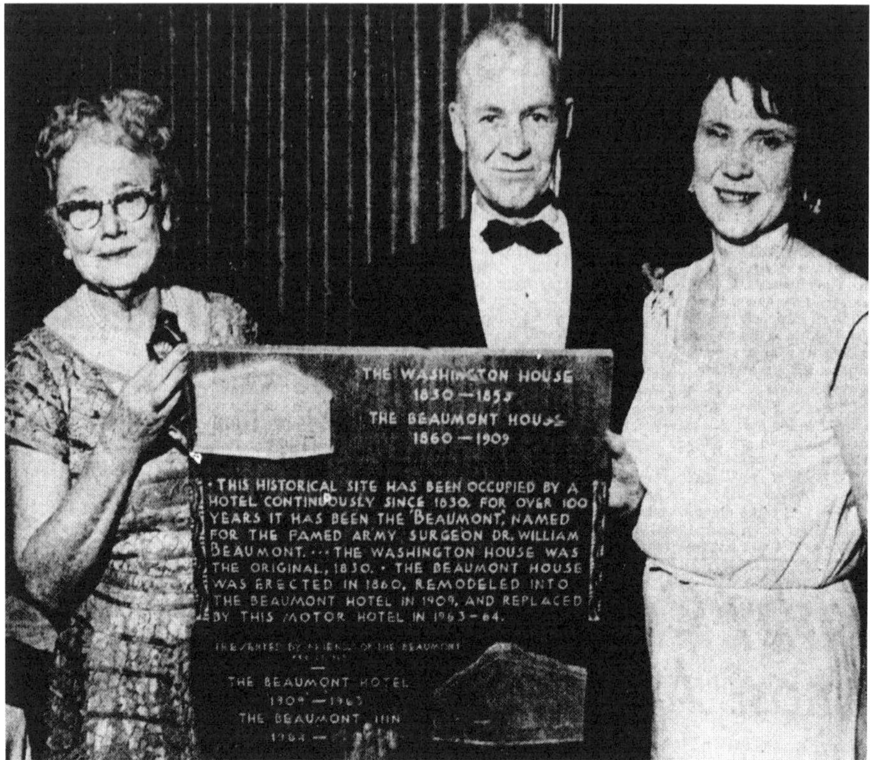

Mrs. A.C. Witteborg and Mr. and Mrs. Carl Witteborg accept a memorial plaque before the hotel was razed in 1963. Press-Gazette *photo*.

Rudolph wrote, "Until the Northland [Hotel] was built in 1923–24, the Beaumont was the city's premier hotel, a distinction it continued to share with the newer house for many years. The celebrities it has entertained and the civic and social events are a story in themselves."

The book *The Green Bay Area in History and Legend* recounted, based on Rudolph's articles, "The Beaumont Motor Inn was sold in 1973 to become the Beaumont Ramada Inn. The Days Inn chain took over the business in 1986, at which time the new owners dropped the familiar and historic Beaumont name."

Chapter 20

THE FIRST BROWN COUNTY COURTHOUSE

After the War of 1812, the population of the Great Lakes region grew. What is now the state of Wisconsin had been part of the Northwest Territory, the Indiana Territory, and the Illinois Territory, and in 1818, it became part of the Michigan Territory. The Michigan Territory was extended west to the Mississippi River, and three counties were subdivided from it: Crawford County in the west, with a county seat in Prairie du Chien; Brown County to the east, with a county seat in Green Bay; and Michilimackinac County to the north, with a county seat in Mackinac.

"The settlers, coming as they did in such numbers after the [war] made the need of a separate territorial government imperative," Wisconsin Superintendent of Schools E.G. Doudna wrote in his 1920 history book, *Our Wisconsin*.

Brown County was organized by the Honorable Lewis Cass, then governor of the Michigan Territory, in October 1818. At the time, the county included the area that is now Kenosha, Racine, Milwaukee, Ozaukee, Sheboygan, Manitowoc, Kewaunee, Door, Walworth, Waukesha, Washington, Fond du Lac, Calumet, Outagamie, Shawano, Oconto, Winnebago, Dodge, Jefferson, Rock, Columbia, Marquette, Waushara, Waupaca, Brown, and a portion of Dane and Green Counties.

Matthew Irwin was appointed as Brown County's chief justice, commissioner, judge of probate, justice of the peace, sheriff, commissioner, and clerk. For five years, prisoners had to be transported by canoe to Detroit for trial.

"It was almost 600 miles to Detroit, the capital of Michigan, and the means of communication were so primitive that the settlers felt it to be as far away as a foreign capital," Doudna stated.

In 1823, Congress passed an act creating an additional judicial district that included Brown, Crawford, and Michilimackinac Counties, and the Honorable James D. Doty was appointed judge. Doty was administered the oath of office on June 30, 1824.

"As early as 1824, Judge James Doty had made an effort to have a separate territory organized. He proposed to call the new territory Chippewa, and he included within its boundaries the northern peninsula of Michigan and a large section of the present state of Minnesota," Doudna said.

Cass approved a county seat to be located within six miles of the mouth of the Fox River. A log building at Menomineeville was selected as the location of the county seat, and Doty traveled between Prairie du Chien, Mackinac Island, and Menomineeville to fulfill his judicial duties between the established counties.

Following the establishment of the Wisconsin Territory, an act was created to change the county seat that read, "That the seat of justice in the county of Brown shall from and after the first day of April 1837, be established with at Navarino, Astor or De Pere, as may be decided by the qualified voters of the said county, as is hereinafter provided."

When the Green Bay vote was split between Navarino and Astor, De Pere saw the majority of the vote and became the county seat. The log courthouse previously used as the courthouse at Menomineeville was then dragged over the ice of the Fox River to De Pere.

The log structure was later replaced by a two-story building on the intersection of the De Pere streets of George and Washington. The first floor held the jail facilities, and the second story contained the courtroom.

De Pere remained the county seat for seventeen years (1837–54). In 1840, court sessions were split between Green Bay and De Pere, with spring sessions held in Green Bay and fall sessions in De Pere.

In 1854, Green Bay was incorporated as a city. Another vote was held to select the location of the county seat, and this time Green Bay won out. The De Pere facility continued to operate as a jail, and the second floor was rented out. The building was also used as a school.

A De Pere Historical Society article stated:

> *Eventually, Brown County sold the building at auction although the local jail continued to occupy the lower level. When the First Presbyterian Church*

organized in 1849 parishioners held services in the old courthouse building until they were able to build their own church in 1854.

In the early morning of March 12, 1871, the De Pere courthouse building burned to the ground. Two locals had been arrested and jailed two days prior on drunk and disorderly charges. One was released the next day but found himself back in jail again that night. He reportedly told the marshal that "he'd be sorry" the next morning for putting him in jail again. The two prisoners perished in the fire.

An inquest following the event found that the prisoner who threatened the marshal may well have set the blaze in an attempt to gain his freedom.

A stone marker erected in 1930 and rededicated in June 2009 now commemorates the location of the first Brown County Courthouse in De Pere.

Chapter 21

OLD BRICK LEADS THE WAY FOR PUBLIC EDUCATION

The Green Bay Area Public School District was founded in 1856 with the establishment of the Sale School. The first city-owned public school was built on the east side of the Fox River at what became 523 Howe Street. At that time, the Fort Howard military base—situated on the west side of the river—offered tuition-based education but functioned independently from the east side.

The Sale School was constructed on land donated by John Jacob Astor, a fur trader who began purchasing land and became more synonymous with New York in later years. Astor founded the town of Astor, which was later united with the town of Navarino to form the city of Green Bay.

The first high school commencement in 1875 had six graduates.

In 1885, the school was remodeled and used solely as a high school.

In Fort Howard, McCartney School opened in 1890 to accommodate high school classes on the west side.

In 1893, East Side High School opened on the corner of Chicago Street and Webster Avenue and became home to secondary education on the east side. At the time, the school was referred to as "the school on the hill," and the student body became known as the Hilltoppers.

"Old Brick"—as the Sale School was affectionately called—was then used as the administrative offices for the district.

In 1895, the Green Bay and Fort Howard districts consolidated, with an agreement to keep a high school on both the east and the west side of the river.

In the early 1900s, the Woman's Club, in an effort to "keep boys interested in going to school," donated funding for some hand tools so the district could offer "manual training." "It was the first vocational subject ever offered in a Green Bay school. Green Bay was not an early bird in the state in this field, but it started the course at a time when there was great interest in the problem of teaching students 'something practical,'" a *Press-Gazette* article stated.

Charles Byrnes was hired to teach the course and given a handful of tools and two rooms in the basement of East High. The course was successful, and mechanical drawing and metalwork were added to the curriculum. Byrnes was soon given two assistants, and the program moved into the Sale School. "It became known as the Sale School of Manual Arts, and the rest of the public schools sent their pupils over for a couple of hours each day," the article said.

The program was later moved to East High when the new school was constructed on Walnut Street.

In 1957, the district offices were moved from the Sale School to the fourth floor of the newly completed Green Bay City Hall. The Sale School building was razed in September 1957.

On November 3, 1957, the First Methodist Church broke ground on the site for a $200,000 addition to their adjacent church facilities. The addition would later house the congregation's offices, Sunday school rooms, and gathering spaces.

Chapter 22

OPENING THE WORLD TO BROWN COUNTY RESIDENTS

In the late 1800s/early 1900s, many entered worlds previously not within their reach when philanthropist Andrew Carnegie created grants to build community libraries.

The National Park Service explained:

> *Between 1886 and 1919, Carnegie's donations of more than $40 million paid for 1,679 new library buildings in communities large and small across America. Many still serve as civic centers, continuing in their original roles or fulfilling new ones as museums, offices or restaurants.*
>
> *The patron of these libraries stands out in the history of philanthropy. Carnegie was exceptional in part because of the scale of his contributions. He gave away $350 million, nearly 90 percent of the fortune he accumulated through the railroad and steel industries.*

Among the communities benefiting from Carnegie's philanthropy was the city of Green Bay—his first grant made in Wisconsin. On February 13, 1901, Carnegie offered the city $20,000 for a library building if the city would furnish a site and provide yearly support of about $2,500. One city lot was donated by Green Bay Bishop Sebastian G. Messmer, and a second lot was purchased by the city.

"Green Bay is in great need of a public library building. The present quarters of the library are small and poorly adapted for the purpose. It is true the library has done excellent service for the city in its present home, but it has long been a settled conviction that a building devoted exclusively to library purposes is an imperative necessity," a February 1901 *Press-Gazette* article stated.

"In 1898, the Women's Club of Green Bay sent out a number of traveling libraries through the county, the books being donated by interested persons. The headquarters were at the Kellogg Library, but at the end of two years, no new books having been donated, the plan was discontinued," Deborah Martin stated in *History of Brown County, Wisconsin—Past and Present.*

As the new building was completed, workers began moving the city's books from the smaller Kellogg Library to the new Carnegie building in early February 1903 and found that their entire inventory, which included reference books stored at the Business College, would not fit on the shelving provided. The bookcases from the old library were then brought in to fill the needed space.

While still dealing with the space needs and other issues, the library set an opening day of February 16, 1903.

"The heating and lighting of the building are not what is desired. The difficulties experienced in the heating some time ago still exist. The power furnished by the Light and Power Company is said to be insufficient to light the building and the matter will be taken up with the company immediately," the *Press-Gazette* said the week prior.

On August 1, 1913, ground was broken on an addition that would double the size of the library, creating one of the "most imposing" public buildings in the city. The addition would include a new children's room, a new librarian's room, and increased room throughout all departments. The library interior was also remodeled during the new construction.

The funding for the addition and remodeling was provided by Carnegie again, with a contingency that the city provide $6,500 in yearly funding this time.

"The city council gave the board permission to sell the house on the lot adjoining the library to the highest bidder," the *Green Bay Semi-Weekly Gazette* stated.

By March 16, 1921, the library was home to thirty-seven thousand volumes—a large portion of them reference in nature—as it worked to keep pace with a growing city, with the city's appropriation growing to $12,000.

By 1925, library revenues sat around $18,000, which was found to be inadequate for its time by American Library Association standards, which suggested $1 per capita. "On a population estimate of 35,000, the sums provided for the Kellogg Public Library have been slightly less than 50 cents per capita, not half as much as the American Library Association considers a minimum basis," a *Press-Gazette* article stated.

By 1926, the library offered 180,210 books. That year, an east wing was added in conjunction with the construction of the Neville Museum facility. The $50,000 project created a joint library-museum facility on the property at Doty and Jefferson Streets.

By 1935, the library was circulating 373,716 books, and by 1941, that number was 491,236.

In June 1966, the Brown County Board of Supervisors endorsed the concept of a county library system, and in 1968, the De Pere and Green Bay library services merged to form the Brown County Library.

In 1974, the central branch of the Brown County Library system moved from the Carnegie building to its current location on Pine Street in downtown Green Bay. The site was renovated into a private facility called Jefferson Court, which is listed on the National Register of Historic Places.

Chapter 23

THE FIRST BANK WEST OF LAKE MICHIGAN

The first bank west of Lake Michigan was created by an act of the Michigan Territory legislature in 1835. Called the Bank of Wisconsin, the bank headquarters were located in Green Bay at the Astor Fur Company trading post, owned by John Jacob Astor and located on the corner of South Washington and Chicago Streets.

"The first effort, I believe, to secure a bank west of [Lake Michigan] was made by Judge Doty on Feb. 14, 1834, when he reported from the committee on corporations a bill to incorporate the Bank of Wisconsin," State Commissioner of Banking Marshall Cousins recalled in 1922 at a Brown County Bankers' Development Association meeting.

On March 4 of that year, the act passed but was vetoed by Michigan Territory Governor George B. Porter on March 7. Cousins said that the governor felt "the establishment of banks in the new and imperfectly organized country was a source of danger" and that he did not think "the necessity for a bank west of Lake Michigan existed."

Cousins stated:

> *He referred to the population as "sparse" and, particularly in the lead mine districts "as unstable" and doubted if a bank could be supported. Gov. Porter referred to the Michigan currency of that day as being "entirely sound" and that he wanted to keep it so.*
>
> *He objected to a requirement that only a majority of the directors were to reside in the county where the bank was to be located while the others*

> *might reside anywhere in the United States; to the provision which allowed the directors to borrow one-fourth of the capital and further objected to the provision for calling a meeting by notice to be printed in a newspaper five weeks previous to the meeting.*

At the time, it was thought that the nearest newspaper was printed in Detroit. Though Wisconsin's first paper—the *Green Bay Intelligencer*—is recorded to have started publication in 1833, it was apparently not on the legislature's radar.

In November of that year, a bill authorizing the organization of a bank in Brown County was introduced by Michigan Territorial Council Member Charles Moran, of Wayne County. The bill passed the legislature on January 20, 1835, and was signed into law by the governor on January 23.

Cousins said:

> *The law named John B. Ansley, John P. Arndt, Charles Tullar, William Dickinson, George D. Ruggles, Henry Merrill and Nathan Goodell as commissioners to receive subscribers and to take the preliminary steps for organization of this bank.*
>
> *The official name of the bank was the "President, Directors and Company of the Bank of Wisconsin." The authorized capital was $100,000 to be divided into 2,000 shares of $50 each and the location of the bank was to be either in the county of Brown or the county of Iowa.*

Of the four existing counties, Michigan Territory 1835 census records show the population in Iowa County at 2,628 and Brown County at 1,958, while Crawford and Chippewa Counties had significantly fewer people.

The *Green Bay Intelligencer* reported on August 22, 1835, that the bill was passed and it was to be "located by a majority of the stockholders. The books were opened at Mineral Point on the second Monday of August last. But a few shares were taken, owing to the uncertainty about the place of operations. The books will be opened at this place on the fourth Monday or August, and from the interest lately manifested, it is expected that the stock will be eagerly taken."

A March 9, 1836 edition of that publication announced a meeting of the stockholders to take place at the home of John P. Arndt later that month "for the purpose of deciding upon the expediency of increasing the capital stock of the bank."

On Independence Day 1836, the Wisconsin Territory was organized, with all current Michigan Territory laws carrying over. In December of that year, a notice was published in the *Wisconsin Democrat* for a meeting to elect the bank's board of directors. The bank would be housed in the Astor Fur Company structure.

"The bank was originally located in a building erected by the Astor Fur Company described as a rambling two-story structure which extended the width of the block and was on the north side of Chicago Street between Adams and Washington streets. The building faced south and looked out on Astor Park," a *Press-Gazette* article stated.

The Bank of Wisconsin collapsed the following year with the Panic of 1837, a financial crisis that began a depression that lasted into the next decade. Investors panicked, and bank customers withdrew their money from the bank.

The large wooden structure that had served as home for the bank eventually disappeared as well; however, the stone bank vault remained until 1899. "The vault was frequently used to preserve the bodies of eastern settlers until arrival of a boat to take them down the lakes for burial," an October 26, 1925 edition of the *Press-Gazette* stated.

Chapter 24

THE LAST LINE OF DEFENSE

In a time before social welfare programs and care facilities, county-run poor farms were the last line of defense when individuals were unable to provide for their own basic needs. Also known as almshouses, the poor houses were tax-supported facilities assisted by a farm in which residents were required to work, if able, in the house or fields in exchange for their room and board. The facilities were operated under the direction of one or more elected officials.

"Up to 1856, several towns cared for their own poor and found it a heavy responsibility and expense, but on March 12, 1856, the board of supervisors decided to abolish this distinction and to make the poor a county charge. The United States government was petitioned to sell private claim 18, on the east side of Fox River, for a poor farm. This property was a part of Camp Smith, and was originally owned by Judge Jacques Porlier. On it stood the old Protestant Episcopal mission house, which the county board hoped to utilize temporarily, but at the November meeting of 1856 the commissioners for the poor reported that they had used their best endeavors to secure the property without success," Deborah B. Martin wrote in the 1913 *History of Brown County, Wisconsin—Past and Present.*

"At the March meeting of 1857, the committee in charge of the county house brought before the board the following offers of land for this purpose: A site on the Fox River, six miles above De Pere, offered by Daniel Whitney for $10 per acre; James Boyd, a farm of 120 acres for $6,000; Paul Fox, one of 129 acres, $2,500; Dr. Israel Green's farm in Ashwaubenon, 140 acres, $5,000; and H.S. Baird's farm of 120 acres for $1,500."

In May 1857, the county board authorized the purchase of 112 acres belonging to David P. Saunders for $1,600. "The property was on the regularly-traveled road to Bay Settlement—the lower road which followed the line of the Bay Shore," Martin wrote.

A house was constructed on the property to accommodate those individuals in need. "The land was good and well adapted to farming purposes and in the course of 10 years was reported as being nearly self-supporting from the fine crops raised there," Martin added.

In June 1874, the Brown County Committee on the Poor House brought forward a recommendation to replace the existing poor house. "The poor house is in bad repair, hardly tenantable, in a leaky condition, and we would recommend a new house to be built at once; being of the opinion that money spent on the old house is money thrown away," the committee reported.

Bids were opened later that month, and the home was completed by the following spring.

"One of the best features of the new poor house is the provision made for the care of the unfortunate insane who have heretofore been confined in the county jail for lack of other suitable place," the *Press-Gazette* stated in August 1875.

The old facility was sold to the highest bidder and removed from the property. The destitute and those with mental health issues were housed here together until 1881, when the county constructed the Brown County Insane Asylum.

In June 1881, a special committee was formed to adopt plans, enter into a contract, and supervise the construction of a building "not to exceed $1,500." The committee received seven bids, with the lowest coming in at $1,955, for which the county provided the needed funding. The new building was completed in December 1881.

In September 1933, the county board held a special meeting to discuss obtaining a loan or grant through the Federal Emergency Administration of Public Works for a new facility.

On November 3, Brown County's application for $300,000 to construct a new facility was approved by the federal public works administration—30 percent an outright grant and the balance through a loan. The county project was one of forty-one nonfederal projects in fifteen states awarded funding that day.

Work was started in 1934 and completed by the end of 1935. The new building created a Y shape, enclosing the original structure between its two wings.

The advent of the Social Security Act in the mid-1930s created provisions for some of the unfortunate who were unable to garner basic necessities, as the facility turned its focus on mental health care and treatments.

In 1948, through an act of the state legislature, the name of the facility was changed to the Brown County Hospital.

In January 1968, another addition was completed with the help of a $675,000 federal construction grant.

In October 1972, the Brown County Board adopted an ordinance for the creation of the Brown County Health Center. "The ordinance, which will bring the treatment of mental disorders, alcoholism and drug abuse under one governing board and a centralized administration, was approved on a 30–12 vote with one supervisor excused," an article in the *Press-Gazette* stated.

In 2002, the county board hit the pause button on a new $32 million facility that had already been approved, opting instead for the idea of privatization. Two years later, a task force recommended killing the idea altogether in favor of downsizing and renovation. In 2005, the county saw the need for the remodeling of the aging facility but fell two votes short of approval. With the cost of renovating estimated at $18,000 to $30,000 and building new $13,000 to $28,000, many may have found it hard to justify.

In October 2006, the county board voted 18–7 to close another section of the mental health center, and in 2009, the mental health center was replaced by a new facility—the Community Treatment Center at 3150 Gerschwin Drive in Green Bay.

In 2010, the county looked for other options in dealing with the 141,000-square-foot mental health facility at 2900 St. Anthony Drive that would cost $1.1 million to demolish. However, with no viable buyer coming forward, the building sat vacant, costing the county $18,000 a year to maintain. In May 2013, the county began seeking bids for the facility's demolition, and that December, workers began to raze the structure.

All that remains of the facility today is the "paupers' graveyard" filled with the unmarked graves of those the county could not identify and placed there and those who once roamed the halls of the poor house.

Chapter 25

THE OLDEST CHURCH IN GREEN BAY

A Wisconsin Historical Society essay stated:

The Moravian Church, an outgrowth of a reform movement in 15th century Bohemia and Moravia, is one of the oldest Protestant bodies in the world. The Wisconsin wilderness was an open invitation to the Moravians who came in the late 1840s and provided the backbone of three distinct Moravian strongholds: Brown and Door counties, Jefferson County and Wood County.

John Frederick Fett, a pioneer missionary for the Moravian Home Missionary Society, was sent to Milwaukee in 1848 and the following year, the first Moravian congregation in Wisconsin was formed among a group of Scandinavians. That same year, 1849, Moravian followers of Norwegian-born Andrew Iverson arrived in Milwaukee, and Fett turned his attention to the German community.

By 1890, there were 1,477 Moravians in Wisconsin, and their numbers increased by 84% in the next decade. Nils Otto Tank and his wife, both missionaries, came to Wisconsin to establish a religious communal colony based on Moravian principles near Green Bay. Tank named it Ephraim and in 1850, Iverson relocated the Milwaukee Moravians to the settlement.

Differences between Tank and Iverson led to Iverson's defection to the shores of Door County where he re-established the community and also called it Ephraim.

But according to a 2002 article written by Paul Brinkmann for the *Press-Gazette*, Iverson was "dismissed as pastor at Fort Howard in 1883 for having an affair with 17-year-old housekeeper and church member Mary Nelson."

"The clergymen separated—Rev. Tank remaining on the west side of the Fox and the Rev. Fett coming over to the east. Thus originated the East and West Side Moravian churches," a July 18, 1934 *Press-Gazette* article stated. Fett conducted the first service in Green Bay on June 9, 1850, the day after he arrived from Milwaukee with the Tanks.

The article continued:

> *Permanent organization of a congregation was not effected until 1851, however, when the Rev. Fett, after another unsuccessful attempt at home mission work in Milwaukee, returned to the city with about 100 Germans* [and] *organized the church.*
>
> *A former parish of the Rev. Fett in New York City contributed about half of the $1,500 collected for the erection of the church edifice, on two lots in the middle of Moravian Street, donated by William B. Astor of New York.*
>
> *On Oct. 20, 1851, the cornerstone of the proposed church was laid...a sturdy example of Colonial architecture with Gothic embellishments to distinguish it from the eastern "prayer meeting" houses.*

Deborah B. Martin wrote in *History of Brown County, Wisconsin—Past and Present*:

> *The Moravian Church on Jackson Square between Madison Street and Monroe Avenue was organized in 1851, with a full membership of 200, and was dedicated in 1852. Rev. J.F. Fett was the first pastor and remained with the congregation for 12 years. This clergyman taught a parochial school to which a number of the English-speaking residents sent their children in order that they might have the advantage of imbibing the German language in the classes of this excellent instructor.*

In the late 1950s, the congregation began planning for a new church, and on December 4, 1960, the cornerstone was laid for a new east-side church at Allouez Avenue and Libal Street. The original church building later served as the Martin Luther Chapel of the Grace Lutheran Church.

In 1972, it was listed on the National Register of Historic Places.

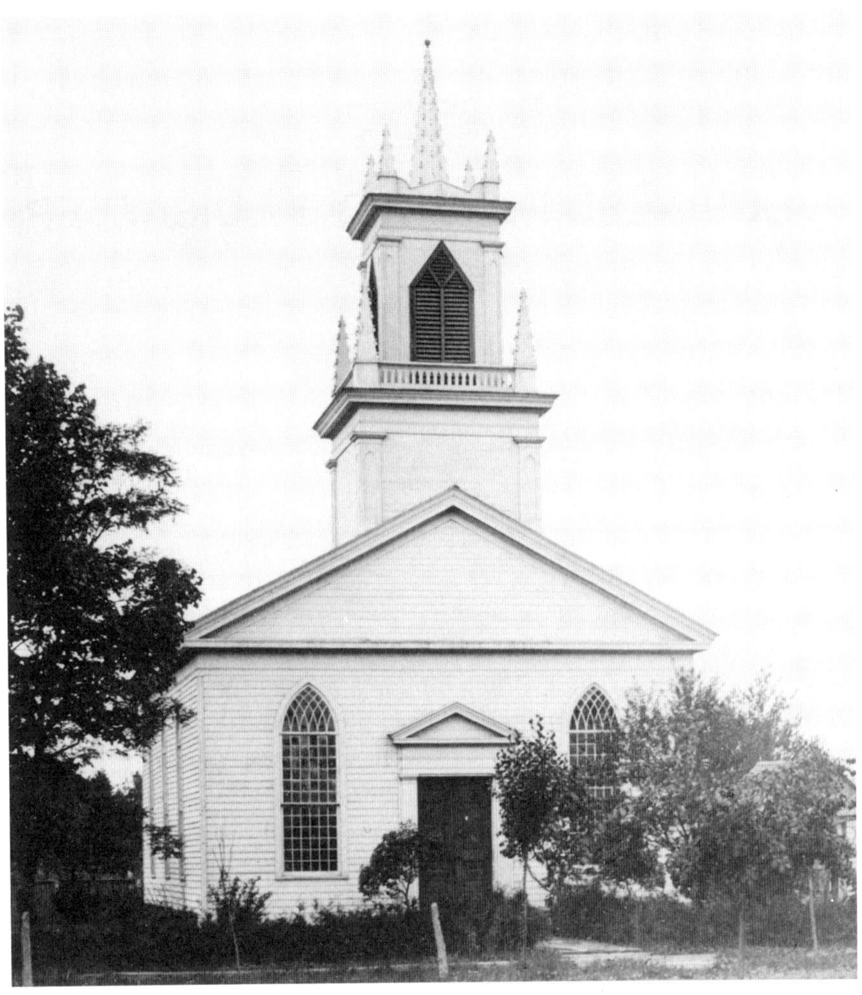

A former parish of the Reverend Fett in New York City contributed about half of the $1,500 collected for the erection of the church edifice, on two lots in the middle of Moravian Street, donated by William B. Astor of New York. *Library of Congress.*

In 1980, the original church was set for demolition, but an anonymous donor stepped forward and provided $150,000 to purchase the building from Grace Lutheran and relocated it for preservation.

On October 20, 1980, 129 years later on the same day and the same hour that the limestone cornerstone was originally laid, the block was placed at the church's future home at Heritage Hill State Park.

The church was rededicated in 1981 and is claimed to be the oldest church building in Green Bay.

Chapter 26

A BUSINESS PLAGUED BY DISASTER

Sebastian Landwehr opened the Green Bay House hotel on the southeast corner of Main and Adams Streets—at 328 North Adams Street—in 1865 and set into motion a business plagued by disaster.

In June 1873, a man was found dead in the hotel with an open bottle of "sulfate of morphine" lying on a table in the room. "An open knife lay on the table with the substance still adhering to the point," the *Press-Gazette* stated.

Days later, a local paper offered up a possible cause to his death as an "unsuccessful love suit." "A number of small trinkets, perfumery, gloves, jewelry, etc., scattered about on the table gives color to the report. His effects will be forwarded to his friends," the *Weekly Gazette* stated.

His remains were interred in the potter's field near the poor farm.

In August 1877, a fire that originated in the Green Bay House barn destroyed the center of the block bordered by Adams, Jefferson, Main, and Pine Streets.

"As to the origin of this fire, Mr. Landwehr thinks that it caught fire in the upper part and was either purposely set or caught fire by a flying spark. He was in the barn 10 minutes before when everything seemed to be all right," a *Green Bay Advocate* article stated.

"Under the circumstances, the fire department did well to save any of the block, which included the Green Bay House, armory and several fine brick stores and residences."

Landwehr had no insurance on the barn but was able to repair it and put it back into operation.

That November, fire struck again, damaging the first and second stories of the hotel. "Nothing positive is known of the origin of the fire," a *Green Bay Advocate* story stated.

But the finger was pointing at a young woman who had been recently dismissed from the hotel. "This girl is of more than questionable character. She was at one time in the Cadie Home but was discharged on account of her loose character. She had recently been discharged from the Green Bay House and it was claimed she was seen leaving the locality where the fire occurred shortly before its discovery," the article volunteered.

As there was insufficient insurance to cover the damage, renovations were slow, but the hotel came back better than ever in 1878.

Then in 1881, the Landwehrs' sixteen-year-old daughter ran off with a hotel employee. While they were later intercepted at a train station, by the time she was returned to the Landwehrs' custody, they had already been married.

From 1887 to 1899, Landwehr was advertising the hotel for sale, but without an interested buyer, he held onto the troublesome property.

Later owners included H.B. Cleereman, John Knaepple, Olaf Anderson, and F.P. Crowley.

On July 12, 1927, the hotel was purchased by the Cady-Barnard Land Company.

"The Green Bay House property, having a frontage of 100 feet on Adams Street and 115 feet on Main Street, is regarded as one of the most desirable business sites in the city," a *Press-Gazette* article stated.

> *At one time, the Green Bay House, which is a two-story structure, was the leading hotel in this city. During its early career, it was the stopping place for many notables and it had a wide reputation because of its excellent cuisine. When the hotel was erected, it was the center of one of the city's nicest residential districts. Soon the march of progress surrounded it with business buildings and within a short time its first-class patronage was taken by the Beaumont Hotel.*

In January 1929, the Cady-Barnard Land Company announced that it would be razing the structure. "Several plans for building on the lot have been considered during the past year, but none have as yet materialized. The occupancy of the building, making a delay necessary to have it vacated, has been considered a handicap in making plans for its permanent use it is said. For that reason, the building has been vacated and will be razed," a *Press-Gazette* article stated.

Chapter 27

A LOST MISSION FOR EDUCATION

In 1823, the Protestant Episcopal Missionary Society established a school in the agency house on Dutchman's Creek (Town of Ashwaubenon), the Rev. Eleazer Williams having charge and Albert G. Ellis conducting the school. Both white and Indian children seem to have attended this school," historian Deborah Martin wrote in *History of Brown County, Wisconsin—Past and Present*.

At that time, both the Episcopal and Catholic churches were engaging in the education of youth.

An attempt was made by the Protestant Episcopal Missionary Society to gather Native American children for the purpose of education, but that met with failure until 1827, when the Reverend Richard F. Cadle was brought in to take charge.

Wisconsin Historical Collections vol. 14, Episcopal Church and Mission in Green Bay 1825–41, noted that the students were slow in coming to the school.

A May 18, 1831 letter from Cadle to P.B. Grignon announced the first student: "I have been happy in receiving your note of this day and with it an accession of a Menominee pupil. I will take good care of him and must solicit to keep his father in good disposition towards this school which he has now."

The mission was established near the old Fort Smith at "Shantytown."

Martin wrote:

> *Possession was obtained from the government of a vacant strip of land....It was a beautiful site, on high ground overlooking Fox River at its broadest stretch, and is included today in the town of Allouez; on it buildings were erected, at a cost of $9,000, and in a year and a half, there were nearly 200 children enrolled and in attendance. Those of pure Indian blood were boarded and clothed as well as instructed free of expense.*

Cadle was aided by his sister, Sarah, and a team of about six teachers. But their mission was soon under the microscope of the community they had aimed to serve.

According to a report to the society's executive committee, "It seems that after children are received, fed, clothed and partially instructed, the parents are apt to claim and take them away. This is a state of things not to be endured, for by it the labors and expenditure of the society may be entirely disappointed."

To remedy that, Cadle suggested incorporation, "so that the indentures which the parents may enter into with the society may have a binding force at law."

"A charge of cruelty was brought against an under teacher of the institution for punishing severely two boys who had been guilty of a serious misdemeanor, and Mr. Cadle sensitively appreciative of the criticism that might include him as head of the institution, resigned after four years of almost insupportable labor and anxiety. In 1842, it was decided by the board of missions to discontinue it as a mission school," Martin said.

"I feel greatly interested in its prosperity and should deeply lament in [if] my withdrawal from it proved the slightest occasion of injury to it. On my own account I am anxious that no children should be removed; and it [if], as opportunity may be given, you would use your influence to prevail upon their parents to allow them to remain, you would confer upon me a great favor," Cadle wrote shortly before his resignation.

In October 1929, a bronze marker was placed at the intersection of Mission Road and Webster Avenue in Allouez to commemorate the approximate site of the first Episcopal mission.

"Although the building, which was destroyed by fire in 1898, was further down the Mission Road, the marker is being placed on the highway, which is state property," the *Press-Gazette* stated shortly before its placement.

The marker was later knocked down and found among rubble near Duck Creek and turned over to the Brown County Historical Society. It was restored and placed on the grounds of the Cotton House at Heritage Hill State Historical Park.

It was later returned to the original site of the mission at 155 West Mission Road, Green Bay, on privately owned property.

Chapter 28

THE MONEY PIT

In 1946, the Green Bay Packers purchased a picturesque fifty-three-acre compound built in 1937 for the Green Bay–area Norbertine order. The $32,000 purchase was approved by the board of directors in May as a "permanent home" for the team.

The *Press-Gazette*'s Art Daley said that the reasons for the acquisition were twofold: "To solve the critical housing situation which the directors fear will last three or four years" and to "give future Packer teams a new and better environment."

"Since the late 1920s, most of the Packers players, especially the single ones, had lived at the Astor Hotel on North Adams Street in downtown Green Bay," explained Packers historian Cliff Christl.

"With its comfortable lobby and connecting bar and barbershop, the Astor served as a welcome center when players arrived in town and a gathering place as long as they stayed.

"With the war coming to an end, more players were starting families and needed more living space."

With short-term rentals hard to find in Green Bay, the team searched for a new home with accommodations to fit the entire team. With three thousand feet of shoreline, a stone gateway, a main hall with dormitory-style bedrooms, a boat launch, tennis courts, and an outdoor theater, along with a hired chef and caretaker, the compound would be a comfortable home at that.

A regulation-sized football field was laid out on the grounds, and a dressing room, equipment room, and showers were added. In July, five cottages were purchased by the Packers Corporation for use by married men and their families.

"[Curly] Lambeau believes he will get the 'absolute maximum' from his players as the result of their new environment since the Packers coach will be able to regulate their diet and better control the after-training activities of the athletes," Daley wrote.

But there was one problem: the grounds were not ideal for a football field. With little topsoil covering the limestone below, the surface wasn't conducive for use as a practice field.

"They held their first practice at Rockwood on Aug. 12, 1946. The next morning, Lambeau was forced to move the workout to City Stadium to save the wear and tear on his players' legs. And it was an ongoing problem," Christl added.

But by essentially paying their players' room and board, Rockwood served as a money pit to some degree. The financial tailspin that the Packers entered in 1946 was largely caused by the formation of the competing All-America Football Conference and the rapidly escalating player salaries resulting from bidding wars over players.

After showing a net profit of more than $23,000 in 1944 and 1945—two of the most lucrative years in their history—it plummeted to less than $4,000 in 1946. Player salaries had increased more than $100,000 from 1944 to 1946, but Rockwood was an additional $15,700 expense in its first year. Lambeau also received a reported pay hike of at least $10,000 in 1945 under a new contract calling for a $25,000 annual salary.

By 1948, the Packers' player payroll had jumped another $45,000, and maintaining Rockwood increased to almost $29,000, leaving the team with a net loss of a little more than $35,000.

"While the concept of Rockwood was visionary, the Packers simply couldn't afford it. Lambeau took much of the heat for the problem because it had been his idea, albeit with the backing of the Packers' wealthy club president Lee Joannes and a board of mostly successful local businessmen," Christl said.

The harmful field conditions at Rockwood Lodge took a toll on some of the Packers players, causing shin splints and other leg issues.

The high cost of decorating the facilities, spearheaded by Lambeau's wife, Grace, caused issues with the Packers Executive Committee, and the absence of the players in the downtown area left local residents disgruntled.

On January 24, 1950, Rockwood Lodge burned to the ground. Sandra and Dan Flagstad, whose parents served as caretakers for the lodge, recalled the sleet- and rain-filled day to the *Milwaukee Journal Sentinel* in 2016. Sandra recalled:

> *Like all kids, we were happy because school was called off. We were upstairs playing, jumping on mattresses. It was winter time, the off-season for the Packers. Only our family was at the lodge.*
>
> *I smelled smoke and heard crackling. I looked at my brother and he opened a door* [to an adjacent room] *and flames gushed out. We ran down the stairway yelling.*
>
> *My dad tried to put it out, but the fire spread so quickly the upstairs was engulfed in flames. We could hear my dad yelling, "Help! Help!" We couldn't get to him because of the fire.*

Sandra's dad had only one way out of the house, jumping from a second-story window, as the others ran to safety.

High winds took the lodge building, which was past the point of saving once firefighters arrived.

After the Rockwood land sat unused for years, Brown County purchased it from the Packers. With money from the United States Land and Water Conservation fund, the county opened Bay Shore Park in 1974.

The insurance policy brought a reported $75,000 to help the financial state of the Packers corporation.

Chapter 29

THE ROUNDHOUSE AND A VISION FOR THE FUTURE

The dream of rails to connect Green Bay with Mississippi River commerce was a concept long before work began on the Green Bay and Lake Pepin Railroad in 1866. "The first meeting of the board of directors of the new railroad was held July 7, 1866," Stevens Point historian Malcolm Rosholt wrote in *Trains of Wisconsin*.

> *There was no lack of interest in the railroad in Brown County, but there was a lack of investment capital for Green Bay, which once thought it might become the leading city of commerce in Wisconsin. It had early on been eclipsed by Milwaukee, which forged ahead of its rival both in commerce and population, and in the process, attracted men of means from the East, or men who knew how to raise additional means, especially to build railways.*
>
> *The railroad investors at Green Bay expected that the line to the Mississippi could be built in less than five years, and there was no reason why it could not have been built in that time, except that not enough money had been subscribed to build the line in one piece so to speak.*

The first spike was driven into a tie on November 3, 1871, in Fort Howard, reaching New London the following year.

The railroad became the Green Bay and Minnesota in 1873 and, in 1881, was sold to the Green Bay, Winona, and St. Paul Railroad.

In 1896, the railway was deeded to the Green Bay and Western (GBW), and a period of reorganization began. "Since the reorganization of the Green Bay & Western company in 1897, a sum of money exceeding $125,000 has been spent in various improvements in this city alone, while a vast amount of money has been expended in a large number of ways on the tracks, the buildings and property of the system," a 1907 *Press-Gazette* article stated.

Improvements included new shops, work on the coal dock, a new depot and freighthouse, and a roundhouse on its property, which extended from Broadway to 12th Street at Mason Street.

By 1908, what became known as the "Green Bay Route" stretched from Marshland Junction on the west side of Wisconsin, south to La Crosse and across central Wisconsin to Green Bay and Kewaunee, and north to Sturgeon Bay.

In 1938, a $4,300 addition was made to lengthen the railroad's Norwood roundhouse to accommodate six new ALCO steam engines.

"Increased traffic during World War II, along with the state's growing industrial base, helped transform the 'two streaks of rust across Wisconsin' into a respectable railroad," the Green Bay & Western Historical Society stated.

However, passenger service declined and finally ended in the late 1940s.

"The car ferries enjoyed their best years in the 1950s, feeding the GBW's traffic base. With few modern steam locomotives, the GBW dieselized in 1950, often paying cash for their new ALCOS instead of financing them," the Green Bay & Western Historical Society added.

> *But the 1960s were a tough decade for the railroad industry as trucks ate into their traffic. Eventually, the younger McGee decided the GBW would be better off as part of a larger system.*
>
> *The Burlington Northern attempted to buy the GBW in 1976, but thanks to resistance from the GBW's neighbors—the Chicago & North Western, the Milwaukee Road, and the Soo Line—the deal was rejected by the Interstate Commerce Commission. Instead, the GBW was purchased by Itel, which owned other railroads and operated a large fleet of freight cars.*
>
> *Thanks mostly to the paper business, the GBW continued to prosper, making it attractive to a larger system. On August 28, 1993, the GBW was purchased by the Wisconsin Central Limited. Its traffic and employees were absorbed by the WC, and the remaining ALCOS were dispersed to other short lines across the U.S. Today, two-thirds of the GBW's mainline remains in service as part of the Canadian National.*

Today, all that remains of the roundhouse that once served as a symbol of progress is the base of the once bustling structure just a short distance west of the Ashland Avenue bridge—a bridge whose activity now overshadows the railroad's existence.

ACKNOWLEDGEMENTS

Many thanks to Deb and Hannah at the UW–Green Bay archives; Mary Jane and Jeff at the Brown County History Room; and Tori, Mike, and Janelle at the *Green Bay Press Times*. Your knowledge and assistance were of great help in piecing together the chapters of this book.

Thank you to my family and friends, especially Mike Warren Kobs, who saw me through a tough year as this book was being put together. This would not have been possible without a strong support system.

And last but not least, thank you to my grandmother, who instilled in me a love of history, as well as a good story.

BIBLIOGRAPHY

Boston Evening Transcript, June 1890.

Brown County History Room archives, 2022–24.

Christl, Cliff. Author interview, 2023.

De Pere Historical Society. www.deperehistory.org.

Doudna, E.G. *Our Wisconsin*. Ulan Press, 2012.

Green Bay Advocate, 1877–85.

Green Bay & Western Historical Society. www.gbwhs.com.

The Green Bay Area in History and Legend. Brown County Historical Society, 2004.

Green Bay Press-Gazette, 1871–2000.

Green Bay Semi-Weekly Gazette, 1899–1915.

Green Bay Weekly Gazette, 1866–99.

Hanson, Reverend John H. "Have We a Bourbon in Our Midst?" *Putnam's Monthly Magazine*, February 1853.

Hinkfuss, Rosemary. Author interview, 2024.

Jones, Marshall B. "Crisis of the American Orphanage, 1931–40." Pennsylvania State University, 1989.

Kalihwisaks, 1980–2020.

Kinzie, Juliette Magill. *Wau-Bun: The Early Day in the Northwest*. Applewood Books, 1873.

Martin, Deborah. *History of Brown County, Wisconsin—Past and Present*. S.J. Clarke Publishing Company, 1913.

Morton, Marian J. "Surviving the Great Depression." John Carroll University, 2000.

Muller, June. Author interview, 2024.

National Park Service. National Register of Historic Places, 2024.

Neville, Ella Hoes. *Historic Green Bay*. Neville, Martin and Martin, 1893.

Resch Center archives, 2024.

Seidl, Bea. *Orphan Doors*. CreateSpace Publishing, 2012.

State Gazette, 1871–94.

Usher, Ellis Baker. *Wisconsin: Its Story and Biography, 1848–1913*. Vol. 8. Legare Street Press, 2022.

UW–Green Bay archives, 2022.

Williams, Eleazer. Eleazer Williams papers, Wisconsin Historical Society.

Wisconsin Historical Collections, 1855–1915.

ABOUT THE AUTHOR

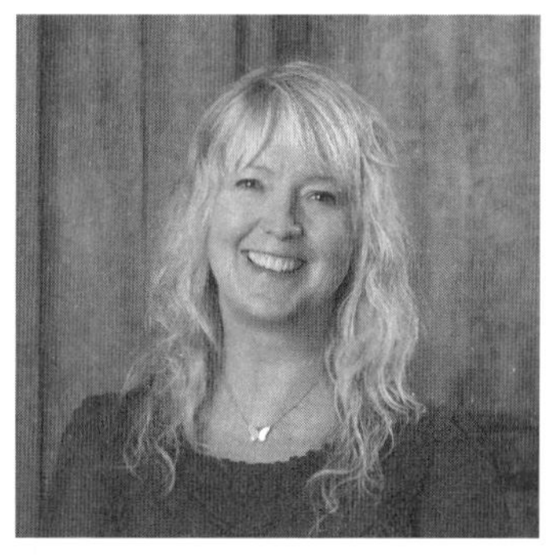

Inspired by the stories her grandmother told her while growing up, Kris Leonhardt has been chronicling North American history since she was a junior in high school.

Leonhardt attended Marquette University and the University of Wisconsin while pursuing a communications degree. She also served in the United States Army, receiving an honorable discharge in 1997.

She began a part-time journalism career in 2001, while working in a family business, and moved to a full-time position in 2006. She now works as senior editor at Multi Media Channels (MMC), owner of more than thirty print publications, including twenty-two weeklies and seventeen digital channels that serve the central, northern, and eastern regions of Wisconsin.

Leonhardt is also a director with the Pass It Forward community journalism internship initiative developed through a partnership with the Green Bay Packers Give Back, Nicolet National Bank, UW–Green Bay, and St. Norbert College, where she helps guide aspiring young writers and journalists.

Through her work on and off the clock, she has been recognized in the communities she serves for historic preservation.